More Praise For
THE American Muslim Teenager's Handbook

"This is a terrific, personable, and useful book for young Muslims and for people of all ages and faiths including the secular, who are still trying to figure out the difference between a great majority of actual American Muslims— real people like the rest of us— and the crazed stereotypes generated by war headlines thousands of miles away. Full of candor, contemporary savvy and wisdom beyond mere years, the *Handbook* should be in the hands and on the minds of inquiring Americans everywhere."
—Michael Wolfe
Author author of *The Hadj & Taking Back Islam: American Muslims Reclaim Their Faith,* and film producer of *Muhammad: Legacy of a Prophet*

"An important contribution for the education of young American Muslims providing important guidelines on becoming American and Muslim."
—Dr. Yvonne Yazbeck Haddad
Professor of the History of Islam and Christian-Muslim Relations, Georgetown University

"I think it's one of the best books for our teenagers and new Muslims. The knowledge of Islam is clear and easy to understand. This book presents an intimate look at the lives of Muslims and the basic beliefs of Islam. HIGHLY RECOMMENDED!"
—Shamshad Sheikh
Associate University Chaplain
Yale University

MORE PRAISE (cont.)

"Being a Muslim teenager in America has become that much easier with the publication of this much-needed and timely book. Written in a highly engaging, non-preachy style, the *Handbook* offers American Muslim teens answers to practically every question that may occur to them concerning lifestyle issues and religious concerns. Strongly recommended for not only these teenagers but their parents as well."
   —Dr. Asma Afsaruddin
      Associate Professor of Arabic and Islamic Studies
      University of Notre Dame

THE american MUSLIM teenager's HANDBOOK

BY
DILARA HAFIZ, IMRAN HAFIZ,
& YASMINE HAFIZ

Acacia Publishing
1366 E. Thomas Rd. Ste. 305
Phoenix, AZ 85014
www.acaciapublishing.com

Library of Congress Cataloging-in-Publication Data

Hafiz, Dilara.
  The American Muslim teenager's handbook / by Dilara Hafiz, Imran Hafiz & Yasmine Hafiz.
     p. cm.
  ISBN-13: 978-0-9792531-2-6 (alk. paper)
  ISBN-10: 0-9792531-2-8 (alk. paper)
  1. Muslim youth--Religious life--Handbooks, manuals, etc. 2. Muslim youth--Religious life--United States--Handbooks, manuals, etc. 3. Muslim youth--Conduct of life--Handbooks, manuals, etc. I. Hafiz, Yasmine. II. Hafiz, Dilara. III. Title.

BP188.18.Y68H34 2007
297.5'70835--dc22
                                        2007010295

Cover design by Yasmine Hafiz
Internal design by Jason Crye
Cover photo of Yasmine Hafiz by Mark Peterman Photography

Printed and bound in China

This book is dedicated to all the teenagers out there who are searching...
Don't give up on your dreams and ideals—may your spirituality guide you to find inner peace and happiness.

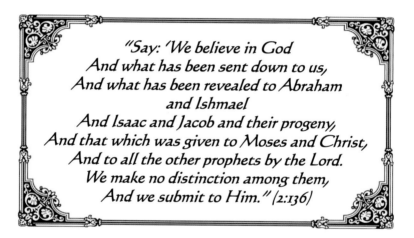

"Say: 'We believe in God
And what has been sent down to us,
And what has been revealed to Abraham
and Ishmael
And Isaac and Jacob and their progeny,
And that which was given to Moses and Christ,
And to all the other prophets by the Lord.
We make no distinction among them,
And we submit to Him." (2:136)

TABLE OF CONTENTS

ACKNOWLEDGMENTS

In the spring of 2002, we mailed out the American Muslim Teenager's Questionnaire (see Appendix 1) to over 40 full-time and weekend Islamic schools in the United States. The results from approximately 150 responses are included throughout the book under the heading *What Do Teens REALLY Think?*. We'd like to thank the following schools for participating: Al Hedayah Academy, Fort Worth, TX, College Preparatory School of America, Lombard, IL, Islamic Foundation School, Villa Park, IL, Islamic Weekend School–Islamic Center of Columbus, Columbus, OH, and Weekend Islamic School–Islamic Center of the North-East Valley, Scottsdale, AZ.

We undertook this project with the goal of reaching out to Muslims and non-Muslims alike by using a non-judgmental, upbeat style. Hopefully this positive format will encourage you to continue your search for knowledge and spiritual guidance wherever it may lead you. We have used Ahmed Ali's 1984 translation of the Quran which is published by Princeton University Press as well as Abdullah Yusuf Ali's 2001 edition of the Quran which is published by Tahrike Tarsile Qur'an, Inc. in Elmhurst, NY.

We'd like to thank all of the many people who have encouraged us along this journey—especially Sister Muna Ali for invaluable corrections, Rabbi Charles Herring for insight into the Jewish faith, and the numerous teens who participated in the survey. Thank you to Asma Gull Hasan and Dr. Jeffrey Lang for their whole-hearted belief in this book and their guidance to American Muslims. We'd especially like to thank Hamid Hafiz, ideal husband and understanding father, for his patience and full-fledged support throughout this project. Most importantly, we'd like to acknowledge our parents/grandparents—Col. M.A.R. Ibn Hafiz & Begum Safia Hafiz and Mr. & Mrs. Bashir and Yvonne Karamali. They epitomize the essence of living a spiritual life and they continue to be stellar examples of the kindness, love, and open-mindedness which unites all faiths as one.

Needless to say, all the opinions expressed in this book, whether by the authors, the teens via the questionnaire, or anonymously, are no reflection upon any of the people or institutions whose names appear within these pages. We take sole responsibility for any errors or misunderstandings we may have inadvertently made.

Imran (14), Yasmine (16), & Dilara Hafiz
May 2006

FOREWORD

by Asma Gull Hasan

Author of
American Muslims: The New Generation,
Why I Am a Muslim: An American Odyssey

"Handbook" – the word reminds you of the Boy Scouts or some other technical, outdoor-type venture. A handbook is meant to be a kind of manual or a guide, to a new place or adventure. So why a "handbook" for American Muslim teens? Because the book you are holding is meant to do that as well. Think of it as a travel guide for a young American Muslim. In which direction should you go? What street should you take? This handbook can't make your decisions for you, but it can give you the tools and judgment every young Muslim – actually, every person – needs to make a decision for themselves. In navigating through the wilds of American culture, balancing it with one's Islamic faith and ethnic heritage, one surely needs a handbook just as much as the Boy Scouts do, maybe more so!

I wish this book had existed when I was a teenager. Instead, I had to figure out the message myself, which I did. But I want better for you, reader. I want you to be able to do more, accomplish more, and achieve more than I or the members of my generation have. To do this, you will need to know what this book contains. The most important lesson to learn is that your Islam is yours, not anyone else's – not your parents', your siblings', or that wacky uncle who lectures you on the Qur'an at every Eid. Be patient with yourself. No one becomes a perfect Muslim overnight. It's a lifelong journey. Even the Prophet Muhammad did not learn of Islam until he was past 40 years old. Do the best you can, and always keep trying.

Now, I know parents might be a little reluctant. It's certainly difficult to turn your teen loose into the wilderness. But that is not what this book is advocating. This book was written by two teens and their mother, too. They discussed the topics that went into the book – both typical and controversial. Their relationship is much stronger for it. Would you rather have your children learn about these things from neighborhood kids? Or would you like them to learn at their own pace, at home, and encouraged by their "handbook" to discuss their questions with you?

There's no magic formula to be a successful teen, but this book is close. Focus on the chapters that interest you most, and re-read them as you need more guidance. Read what other kids your age had to say about the same things, and use this book as a springboard to discuss these issues with your parents and friends. Good luck!

Asma Gull Hasan
September 2006

PREFACE

The idea for this book began innocently enough. My daughter and I were in a bookstore a few years ago. I wandered past the 'Bargain Books' section while she made a beeline to the Young Adults/Teen section. After browsing, selecting a few books, and making our purchases, she remarked to me, "Mom, why aren't there any books for Muslim teenagers? I saw some interesting ones for Christian teens – I wish there was one for Muslim teens, too." I didn't have a good answer for her. A few weeks later, my son related an incident in his middle school where a group of kids labeled him as a member of the 'Taliban.' Despite assertions to the contrary, he was unable to convince them, as they were certain that all Muslims believed in an extremist version of Islam. His frustration was palpable as he remarked to me, "I wish there was something I could give them that would basically explain Islam to them – not a boring textbook, but something interesting!"

As a mother of two teenagers, I know from personal experience that young adults are full of curiosity and are inclined to ask "Why?" before doing what they're told. As a Muslim in America, I also realize the unique challenges and opportunities facing these teens. In a way, Muslim teenagers are poised to enjoy the best of all possible worlds. They are free to practice their religion in a multi-religious country. They can also tap into the rich cultural heritage of their ancestors by joining international clubs, speaking different languages, and enjoying the cultural diversity that defines America. But too often Muslim teens are confused or ignorant about their own religion, whether by choice or lack of opportunity.

This handbook seeks to stimulate and educate, but in no way purports to be a definitive guide to Islam. The study of any religion can require a lifetime of dedication. Islam is a religion which is over 1,400 years old. While countless scholars have studied and defined the myriad facets of Islam, I have chosen to address the specific topic of Muslim teenagers in America from the perspective of Muslim teens themselves. By choosing such a specific, but often overlooked, audience, my teenagers and I are hoping to grab the attention of a section of American Muslims by engaging them in a dialogue about teen issues and concerns. I strongly encourage any reader to further their education by reading more books about Islam, or better yet, pick up the Quran and study it. My children and I have written this book with the best of intentions – to let Muslim teenagers all over America know that they are not alone or forgotten. God willing, anyone who picks up this book will benefit from a little of the wisdom and truth which is quoted from teenagers from all walks of life.

Dilara Hafiz
May 21, 2006
Paradise Valley, Arizona

INTRODUCTION

How many times have you heard your parents say "Why can't you be more like_____??" (Fill in the blank with either 'your sister,' 'your cousin,' or 'Mrs. So and So's son.') Or the ever popular "When are you going to grow up?" Being a teenager is exciting, challenging, and at times, confusing, but growing up as a Muslim teenager in America can seem an overwhelming task. Where do you go for answers? To whom can you turn to for advice? While your parents, teachers, and friends are all sensible choices, sometimes the topics seem too important to trust to impromptu discussions.

Religion is just one of those topics – serious, important, maybe even 'uncool,' but also essential to the spiritual well-being of any God-conscious person. Teenagers and religion?? At first glance, maybe these two concepts don't seem to fit together at all. But who needs factual, down-to-earth advice more than an American Muslim teenager facing peer pressure, hormonal mood swings (pimples included free of charge!), and the demands of an ever-changing society?

While several excellent books offering guidance to parents of teenagers are currently on the market, there is a dearth of information written by teens, for teens, and most importantly, in an easy-to-read, teen-friendly format. Have a question about prayer? Turn to Chapter 3 and check out the accompanying 'How to Pray' section. Confused about the etiquette of fasting? Chapter 5 will fill in the gaps in your knowledge while keeping your mind off your hunger pangs. The results of the American Muslim Teenager's Questionnaire will surprise you, hopefully not bore you, and possibly encourage you to learn more about Islam and other faiths.

Whether you're an experienced Muslim, new to religion in general, or just curious about Muslim beliefs, this book will provoke you. Keep an open mind and an open heart, for God loves those who search for knowledge. Islam is the fastest growing religion in America, and the most misunderstood. By answering some basic questions and reviewing widespread Islamic beliefs, this handbook will equip Muslim teens in America with the self-confidence to face the post-9/11 world they find themselves in, as well as initiate an interfaith dialogue with like-minded readers. So go ahead and find a topic that interests you – read on!

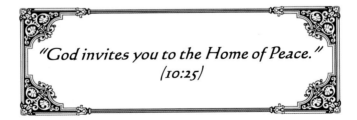

"God invites you to the Home of Peace."
[10:25]

CHAPTER 1

Islam 101
An Overview of the Beginning

> *"All those who believe,*
> *And the Jews and the Sabians and the Christians,*
> *In fact anyone who believes in God*
> *and the Last Day,*
> *And performs good deeds,*
> *Will have nothing to fear or regret."* (5:69)

Islam is the name given to the message revealed to the Prophet Muhammad in 610 AD in a small city in Saudi Arabia. He continued to receive revelations from God transmitted by the Angel Gabriel over the next 23 years. The word 'Islam' literally means 'submission' or 'peace,' and in the context of religion, it is commonly defined as 'one who finds peace through submission to God.' Islam is the second largest religion in the world after Christianity, with over 1.3 billion followers. Muslims come from many different ethnic backgrounds, bringing with them varying customs, languages, and cultural nuances in practicing their common faith. Thus

Islam in practice is a colorful and fluid tapestry made up of interesting people from all walks of life sharing common beliefs and common values. In reality, there is no such thing as an 'average Muslim.' For example, your Muslim neighbor is just as likely to come from Bangkok, Thailand as he is from Boise, Idaho!

Why did Islam originate in the Middle East six centuries after Jesus Christ? Muslims believe that God has been sending the same essential message since the days of Adam and Eve. He has been asking us to believe in Him, worship only Him, and live righteously on Earth in the knowledge that we will someday return to Him. Pretty simple message, right? So how and when did we go astray? Why are there so many different religions when many of them have so much in common? Well, for a start, God rarely gave His instructions in writing. There's a reason for the instructions on bottles of shampoo – "Lather, rinse, repeat as needed." We need guidance for the littlest things in life, so it makes sense that we need the instructions for life in writing. Maybe if Adam had had a handy little pocket guide to refer to in times of doubt, he and Eve would have ignored Satan's whispers of temptation which encouraged them to sample the one tree in the garden that God had forbidden to them. However, it's not appropriate to second-guess God. He eventually gave His game plan in writing (the Sacred Scrolls) to Abraham, arguably the first monotheist who shunned the worship of idols.

Abraham lived about four thousand years ago (1800 BC) in the Mesopotamian Valley. His father was a maker of the idols and statues which the people of that community worshiped. Abraham, however, questioned his people's beliefs and attempted to show them the futility of worshipping idols. He further demonstrated through analogy that it is foolish to worship a star, the moon, or the sun as all these heavenly objects disappear from sight during various times of a 24-hour day. It was an incredible leap of faith for him to convince his community to place their faith in the worship of an unseen God. However, after many trials and even ostracism, the strength of Abraham's conviction managed to sway the majority of his peers. Muslims believe that in the ensuing years, Abraham and his son, Ishmael, rebuilt the

The Kaabah in Mecca

Kaabah in Mecca, Saudi Arabia, the first building dedicated to the worship of the one God which was originally built by Adam.

Thus Abraham is viewed in a religious context as the first monotheist and the patriarch of Judaism, Christianity, and Islam. These three 'Abrahamic' faiths, as they have come to be known, can all trace their roots back to Abraham. His story is described in the Old Testament as well as in the Quran. Muslims trace their ancestry back to Abraham through his son Ishmael, while Jews trace their lineage back to him through his second son, Isaac. The similarities in Abraham's message when viewed through the individual lenses of these three religions is remarkable – confirming Abraham as their common ancestor emphasizes to Muslims the belief that God has been sending the same message to mankind, yet man himself forgets or changes His words.

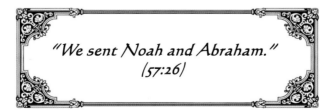

"We sent Noah and Abraham."
[57:26]

5

Muslims accept the notion that God selected various people throughout history to receive His message in written form. In Islam, these prophets are referred to as 'messengers'.

Messenger	Book
Abraham/Ibrahim	Scrolls
Moses/Musa	Torah
David/Dawud	Psalms
Jesus/Issa	Gospel
Muhammad	Quran

In addition to these messengers, God chose numerous men as His prophets to teach the people how to grow closer to God through living a righteous life on Earth. Countless prophets from the Old Testament also appear in the Quran, including Adam, Noah, Jacob, Solomon, Jonah, and Aaron, to name a few. Hence the body of historical fables is strikingly similar in all three religions, and Muslims revere all these prophets and their received books as divinely inspired by God.

How and when did Islam originate if God had already revealed His message to mankind several times in the past? Although Judaism and Christianity were quite widespread by the sixth century, Muslims believe that their practice had begun to differ from the initial message, perhaps as a result of political and social influences from the surrounding communities. Thus it was necessary for God to resend the same message through a different messenger, this time in writing and in Arabic so that the people of that place (Arabia) could understand it for themselves. (Muslims believe that the message of the Quran is a basic message for all humanity, therefore numerous translations of the Quran exist throughout the world.) Previous messages had been revealed in Hebrew or Aramaic, both languages which had changed significantly over the years, resulting in discrepancies creeping into the numerous translations at that time.

Islam recognizes Muhammad as the last chosen messenger in the year 610 AD. A pious man to begin with, Muhammad was distressed at the rampant materialism and inequalities he observed in Meccan society around him. His contemplative nature led him to retreat periodically to a cave in the nearby mountains in order to meditate on the meaning and

purpose of life. It was during one such retreat that Angel Gabriel appeared to him and instructed him to 'Read.' Thus began a series of revelations which continued for the next 23 years. Muslims believe that Muhammad is the 'Seal of the Prophets,' which means that God no longer needs to send another messenger as this time His message is contained in written form in the Quran. The essential message remains the same – to believe in the one God, to worship Him, and to do as many good deeds as possible in order to be reunited with God in the hereafter.

Besides the 22 Arab countries, there are another 35 countries with Muslim-majority populations. This total of 57 countries represents about one-third of the total 191 independent countries in the world.

Fundamentally, Judaism, Christianity, and Islam have far more in common with each other than any of the other world religions such as Hinduism, Buddhism, or Sikhism. Ultimately, all religions are a roadmap to life. Whether we choose to stay on the path or explore side roads is entirely up to us, but we may be pleasantly surprised to learn that we all end up at the same destination.

7

Children of Abraham

Judaism	Christianity	Islam
Abraham (1800 BC)	Jesus (29 AD)	Muhammad (610 AD)
Belief in God	Belief in God as Trinity	Belief in God
The Torah (Hebrew Bible)	The Bible	The Quran
One earthly life	One earthly life	One earthly life
Day of Judgment	Day of Judgment	Day of Judgment
15 million people	2.1 billion people	1.3 billion people

You've probably heard people refer to 'The Five Pillars of Islam.' Do they summarize the faith? Most Muslims are taught the five pillars (see below) at an early age, but once they begin reading the Quran, they're often surprised to learn about all the other aspects of their religion. The essential message of kindness, goodness, and righteousness is evident on each page of the Quran. Focusing on the belief in the one God and performing as many good deeds as possible are the two vital elements repeated *most often* in the Quran. There are varying degrees of observance of the five pillars in any Muslim society - American Muslims are no different from any other faith group in their variety. So don't judge everyone you meet according to your standards or understanding of their religion - sometimes outward appearances can be deceptive. Millions of people of all faiths are good people who practice love, charity, and community service without their neighbors being aware of their actions!

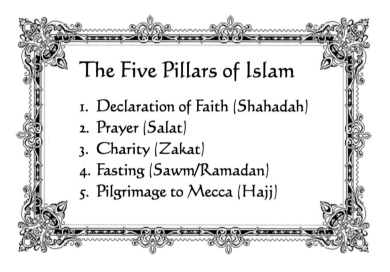

The Five Pillars of Islam

1. Declaration of Faith (Shahadah)
2. Prayer (Salat)
3. Charity (Zakat)
4. Fasting (Sawm/Ramadan)
5. Pilgrimage to Mecca (Hajj)

NOTES

CHAPTER 2

Shahadah
Islam's Central Belief

> *"There is no compulsion in matter of faith.*
> *Distinct is the way of guidance now from error.*
> *He who turns away from the forces of evil*
> *And believes in God, will surely hold fast*
> *To a handle that is strong and unbreakable,*
> *For God hears all and knows everything."* [2:256]

W hat does it mean to be a Muslim? Ask 10 people and you'll probably receive 10 different answers. The standard criteria is 'one who submits to the will of God'. In plain English, that translates to believing in God. Most Muslims would say that uttering the Shahadah, (also known as the 'Declaration of Faith' or the 'Islamic Creed') at least once in one's life qualifies a person to call himself a Muslim. Following is a transliteration of the Shahadah and an English translation:

'Ash-shadu an la ilaha illallah wa Muhammadur rasulullah'

'I bear witness that there is no god but God, and that Muhammad is His Messenger.'

The emphatic assertion that there is only one God serves to highlight this most central belief of Islam; indeed the declarative 'no god but God' rules out the belief in idols or a pantheon of Gods such as the early Roman and Greek fundamentals of mythology. The statement also includes the fact that Muhammad, while the last prophet, was only a messenger/man, not a divine entity in and of himself. This belief that Muhammad was a human being, born of the flesh of a man and a woman, who was capable of error and human weakness, also instructs Muslims that no one is perfect. Only God is All-Knowing, Divine, and Perfect.

The Shahadah is beautiful in its simplicity, but being a Muslim involves more than reciting this phrase once in a lifetime or only on Fridays or even 17 times a day. Being a Muslim is a way of life. By promising to 'bear witness,' you are declaring that you will live your life in the belief that God sees your every action, knows your innermost thoughts, and is ever-present in your life. This state of 'taqwa' or 'God-consciousness' greatly simplifies your life as it gives you a guide (God), with the Quran as your road-map. In other words, when in doubt, do the right thing.

Trusting that God is in your life will enable you to be more confident, more observant, and more humble – a unique combination which many people, both Muslims and non-Muslims, constantly aspire to, but few actually achieve. The foundation of the Judeo-Christian-Islamic belief system is the belief in the one God. That He is the same God may surprise some people, but the reality is that all three religions refer to the same God.

12

Why Are YOU a Muslim?

50% – Because my parents are.
20% – Because of my beliefs/Because I believe in the teachings of Islam.
15% – Because it's cool. Muslims rock!
15% – Because the more I learn about it, the more I realize that I really am a Muslim.

The Inside Scoop – What Do Teens REALLY Think?

Arooj (14), Ohio: "Truthfully, I started out as a Muslim by name which I got from my parents, but over time I realized Islam was really what's right for me. That is when I believe I became a Muslim by heart and not simply by name."

Maymuna (11), Texas: "Because I understand Islam, and it's so clear."

Faraz (15), Ohio: "I was born a Muslim, so I have an advantage because I have been taught Islam while having an open mind. I am a Muslim because this religion makes sense, while having logical guidelines."

Liza (16), **Illinois:** "I was Christian, then I converted when I felt the time was right. That was when my heart was in it. I am a Muslim because I want to be. I feel that it is the only religion that truly serves Allah."

Amira (16), **Ohio:** (*Thank you, Ohio, for all your responses!*) "This is a difficult question. I was born a Muslim, but did not fully embrace Islam until I was 14 years old. I was a sophomore in high school, and at the beginning of the year I was still wearing short skirts and t-shirts. Something happened to make me realize that I was doing something wrong, and I started being more modest and praying 5 times daily. My parents never forced me to become a Muslim – they let me realize it on my own, and I love them for that."

Julia (12), **Arizona:** "Because of the beliefs and what the religion is all about."

How Strong Is Your Faith??

1. Your geography teacher mistakenly identifies Mecca as a city in Iraq. You...
   a) Slide lower in your chair and pretend to be fascinated by the interior of your desk
   b) Tentatively whisper to your neighbor, "I think he means it's in Saudi Arabia – or somewhere over there."
   c) Frantically wave your hand in the air to correct the error.

2. Your whole class is excitedly preparing for the annual Christmas play. You...
   a) Pretend you have a doctor's appointment during rehearsals – every Tuesday and Thursday afternoon for the next two months!
   b) Explain to your teacher that while you don't feel comfortable being an actor, you'd be happy to help out with costumes or set design.
   c) Try out for the part of the camel (either end) and hope that your parents won't recognize you beneath all that fake fur.

3. Everyone is excited about attending the prom, but you're not allowed to go because it requires a date. You...
   a) Loudly protest about the amount of time and money that is commonly spent on prom preparations
   b) Realize that this event is important to your friends, so you offer to help with decorations and set-up, then spend the evening at home with your family.
   c) Politely refuse to accept any dates and explain that in Islam, physical contact between unmarried people (such as slow dancing) is frowned upon, but you try to get a group of friends to go together 'as friends.'

4. You went to the morning prayers on Eid, so you're late to school. Everyone asks, "Where were you?" You...

    a) Tell them that you had a dentist appointment (and pretend that your cheeks are numb with Novocaine).

    b) Proudly declare to the class, "I was at Eid prayers!", then explain that holiday's significance in your religion.

    c) Pretend that you've temporarily gone deaf.

5. Your school is preparing for an inter-faith assembly and asks for volunteers to speak on stage about their religions/ beliefs. You...

    a) Ignore the announcement and hope no one volunteers you.

    b) Take charge of the event and delegate random people to research and present a variety of different religions.

    c) Volunteer to explain your beliefs in an interesting and informative manner.

6. You overhear a group of ignorant bullies jeering at some other Muslim students who are fasting during Ramadan. You...

    a) Ask your principal to make an announcement over the PA explaining Ramadan.

    b) Tell the bullies that they should try fasting to lose some of the fat that is clogging up their brains – then run!

    c) Pretend that the rules of Ramadan don't apply to you while you chow down in the cafeteria with your friends.

ANSWERS

1. At least 'b,' but 'c' if you're brave enough – It's not easy correcting the teacher, but world geography is important.
2. 'b', although 'c' would be pretty funny. Actually, there's nothing wrong with participating in celebrating someone else's religion from an inter-faith point of view. It doesn't mean that you accept or believe in it, so if you enjoy acting, go right ahead.
3. Definitely not 'a' – you'll alienate your friends unnecessarily. Either 'b' or 'c' should be fine if you clear it with your parents first.
4. 'b,' because it's the truth, plus 'a' would be an embarrassment during lunch because you'd have to dribble your drink out of one side of your mouth to keep up the dentist story!
5. 'c' if preferable, but 'b' would be ok, too, as that way everyone would learn something about a different religion by actually researching it, rather than just listening to someone speak about it.
6. Only choose 'b' if you're on the track team, otherwise 'a' is the way to go.

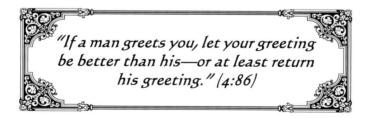

"If a man greets you, let your greeting be better than his—or at least return his greeting." (4:86)

NOTES

CHAPTER 3

Prayer
All Your Prayers Answered

> *"Your only friends are God and His Messenger,*
> *And those who believe and are steadfast*
> *in devotion,*
> *Who pay regular charity and bow in homage*
> *[before God]." [5:55]*

T he most important belief in Islam is the belief in the one God. (By the way, 'Allah' means 'God' in Arabic. Simply 'God,' not a Muslim God or an Arab God – just 'God.') Allah is God – the same God that Jews and Christians all over the world worship. Monotheism, the belief in one God, is the central tenet of all the three Abrahamic faiths – namely Judaism, Christianity, and Islam. They're referred to as 'Abrahamic' because they all look to Abraham as the first person who worshipped the one God. Traditionally, Muslims include Adam as the first prophet in a long line of prophets (believers in the one God). However, Abraham is recognized for his role in turning away from polytheism towards monotheism, and therefore his name has been conferred upon the three main monotheistic faiths.

So that there is no confusion in anyone's mind, God will be referred to as God from now on as this book is in English. However, if it were translated into Arabic, 'Allah' would be the word of choice, just as 'Dieu' would be selected for the French translation, or 'Dios' in the Spanish translation, etc.

The Quran has several themes that are repeated throughout its pages. The most obvious one is the belief in God. On almost every page, God is asking us to believe in Him, to worship only Him, and to have faith in Him. Assuming that no one has a problem with believing in God, let's move on to another important theme – prayer. God continually reminds us to pray, but He doesn't need our prayers, does He? Why should we pray to someone we can't see or get a response from? Good questions – now let's search for some answers.

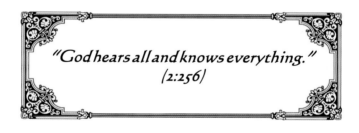

"God hears all and knows everything."
[2:256]

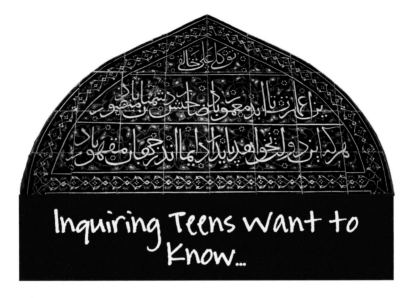

Inquiring Teens want to Know...

1. *What is prayer?*

   Talking to God. In Islam, prayer most often refers to the required 5 daily prayers which consist of 'rakas' or units of prayer. The prayer is memorized and recited in Arabic. However, you can also recite a prayer or supplication whenever you feel like it, in whatever language you feel comfortable with (like English!), and wherever you happen to be, ie, sitting in the car, in class before a test, before you begin a meal, etc.

2. *Do I have to pray?*

   No one can force you to pray – remember, no compulsion in religion, but if you believe that God wants you to pray, you will. Don't pray if you're doing it out of guilt or fear or parental pressure, pray because you truly want to.

3. *Am I still a Muslim if I don't pray?*

   Yes, of course. *Being a Muslim is a state of mind, and no one knows what's in your heart other than you and God.* Don't pray to impress others – do it for God.

21

4. *I don't know how to pray – help!*

No problem – open to the handy 'How To Pray' section and keep the book on the floor in front of you while you pray. Pretty soon you'll have the basics memorized and will be praying like a pro.

5. *Does each prayer of the day have a special name?*

Yes. In order, the names of the prayers are Fajr, Zuhr, Asr, Maghrib, and Isha.

Five Reasons to Pray

1. God asks us to.
2. Parents tell us to – but they need to first teach us how to!
3. We should give thanks for our blessings.
4. It makes us feel better inside (not the 'hot chocolate with mini-marshmallows on a cold day' good feeling, but the 'I found $20 and turned it in to the lost and found' good feeling.)
5. It's the right thing to do.
6. It can't make your life any worse, but it may make your life a lot better.

(Yes, there are six reasons listed, not five, but then you can probably think of many more... See, this prayer thing may be easier than it seems.)

Do Teens REALLY Pray? Honestly??

Samiah (11), Arizona: "I do pray every maghrib prayer in the month of Ramadan and when we go to special prayers for funerals. I don't pray five times a day all the time because I haven't memorized some parts, but I plan to memorize them soon."

Sumbul (14), Illinois: "It's really weird. I have months when I seriously won't miss a single prayer. And then there will be times when I'll miss two or three prayers all together. Isha and Fajr are the hardest, but I feel the best after praying them."

Anonymous (14): "Yes, I miss a few daily... only because I am so lazy... but I try and make them up."

Bashirah (15), Illinois: "Yes, I do pray. I usually pray only three of the five prayers, because for some reason it no longer feels as holy or spiritual. It's feeling more like a chore, and sometimes I get mad at Allah for not being there like He said He would if you're a true believer and pray, etc. So I guess I don't believe in it as much. But I pray three times a day just in case."

Anonymous (16): "I will not lie — not regularly. I know it's wrong and that I should be praying, but my laziness takes over. I'm trying to improve on that."

Amira (16), Ohio: "Yes, I do pray a minimum of five times a day. If I'm feeling particularly happy or sad that day, I'll do extra."

Reyhan (16), Ohio: "I pray five times a day because it says in the Quran that you should be steadfast in prayer. I believe that if you are not steadfast in your prayer, you will forget Allah."

Lots of Anonymous (All Ages), All States: "No — I don't know how," or "No — I don't know why not."

Although the Quran does not specify the actual prayer times, there are numerous references in which God asks us to bow in worship to Him before sunrise, when the sun is at its peak, during the sun's decline "from the meridian to the darkening of the night," after sunset, and late at night (17:78). Thus Muslims follow these instructions to the best of their ability, basically emulating the manner in which Prophet Muhammad taught his early followers to pray. It would be a fallacy to assume that each and every Muslim observes the obligatory five daily prayers; however, it is important to remember the reason behind the emphasis on regular, daily prayer. Formulating good habits can keep you focused on your life goals and instill obedience while also giving structure to your daily life. However, sometimes quality can outweigh the benefits of quantity. For example, if you are only able to pray once or twice a day, or even once or twice a week, but you really concentrate on your prayer and truly try to honor God, then who is to say that you are less pious or 'good' than someone who prays five times a day, but does so unthinkingly out of habit? It's like the difference between a slow connection to the Internet which you have to repeatedly dial up for each little thing versus a high-speed connection which  downloads data faster and more accurately, so you only have to log on occasionally. Obviously, the Quran is beseeching all believers in God to pray as often as possible for their own well-being/peace of mind, but each of us is an individual on his own spiritual journey... only God can judge the sincerity of our prayers. There is no official clergy or priesthood in Islam – the emphasis is on a direct connection between the individual and God.

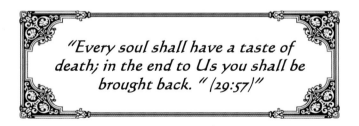

"Every soul shall have a taste of death; in the end to Us you shall be brought back. " (29:57)"

NOTES

HOW TO PRAY:
A STEP-BY-STEP GUIDE

1. Perform 'Wudu' (ritual cleansing). See the glossary at the end of this section for a full explanation.

2. Stand upright on a clean surface and face the direction of the Kaabah (Qiblah). See the prayer glossary at the end of this section for an explanation of Qiblah and the Kaabah.

3. State your intention (Niyah – see the prayer glossary below).

4. Raise your hands to your ears and say, "Allahu Akbar." ("God is Great.")

5. Cross your hands in front of your chest and recite "Surra al-Fatiha" ("The Opening") in Arabic as follows:

"Bismillahir rahmanir rahim.
Al hamdu lil lahi rabbil alamin.
Arrahmanir rahim
Maliki yawmiddin.
Iyyaka na 'budu wa iyyaka nasta 'in.
Ihdinas siratal mustaqim.
Siratal ladhina an 'amta
'alaihim,
Ghairil maghdubi alaihim
Wa lad daallin." (1:1-7)
Ameen.

(Translation)
"In the name of God, Most Gracious, Most
Merciful.
All praise be to God, Lord of all the worlds,
Most Gracious, Most Merciful;
King of the Day of Judgement.
You alone we worship, and to You alone we turn for
help.
Guide us to the straight path,
The path of those You have blessed,
Not of those who have earned Your anger,
Nor those who have gone astray."
Amen

6. Recite another surra from the Quran. For
example, "Surra al-Ikhlas" ("Purity"):

"Qul hu wal lahu ahad,
Allahus samad,
Lam yalid wa lam yulad,
Wa lam ya kul lahu kufuwan ahad."
(112:1-4)

(Translation)
"He is God, the One the Most Unique,
God, the Eternal, Absolute;
He has begotten no one,
And is begotten of none;
There is no one comparable to Him."

7. Bend down from the waist (Ruku), saying "Allahu Akbar" ("God is Great"). Place your hands on your knees, and say, "Subhana Rabbiyal Azim" ("Glory to my Lord, the Great") three times.

8. Stand up from the bowing position and say, "Sami Allah huliman hamidah. Rabbana wa lakal hamd." ("Allah hears those who praise Him. Our Lord, praise be to You.") This standing position is called 'Qiyam'.

9. Say "Allahu Akbar" ("God is Great") while prostrate upon the floor with your knees, forehead, nose, and palms touching the

30

floor. Recite "Subhana Rabbiyal A'la" ("Glory to my Lord, the Highest") three times. This position is called 'Sajdah'.

10. Sit upright on your knees with your palms placed on them while saying "Allahu Akbar" ("God is Great"). After a moment's rest, prostrate yourself upon the floor again, repeating "Subhana Rabbiyal A'la" ("Glory to my Lord, the Highest") three times again. This short sitting in between the two prostrations is called 'Jalsah'.

11. Get up while saying "Allahu Akbar" ("God is Great"). This completes one 'rak'ah' or unit of prayer. The second rak'ah is similar to the

first, except a different short surra is recited after the "Surra al-Fatiha.".

12. Following the second prostration, a longer 'Jalsah' is performed while repeating the following prayer called 'At-Tashahhud:'

"At-tahiyyatu li-Llahi
Wa-s-salawatu wat-tayyibatu
Assalamu 'alai-ka 'ayyuhu-n-nabiyyu
Wa rahamtu-lahi wa barakatu-Hu
'Assalamu 'alaina
Wa 'ala ibadilLahi-s-salihin
'Ashhadu 'an la illaha 'illa-Llahu
Wa 'ashhadu 'anna Muhammadan
'Abdu-Hu wa rasulu-Hu"

(Translation)
All prayer is for God
and worship and goodness
Peace be on you, O Prophet
and the mercy of God and His blessings
Peace be on us
and on the righteous servants of God
I bear witness that there is no God but God
and that Muhammad is His servant and messenger.

When you recite the 'Ashhadu 'an la' section of the prayer, you raise your right index finger up from your knee in symbolic remembrance of the one God.

13.After the 'Tashahhud,' you recite an additional prayer called 'Darud' which confers blessings on Prophet Muhammad and Prophet Abraham in particular. The 'Darud' is as follows:

"Allahumma salli 'ala Muhammadin
Wa 'ala 'ali Muhammadin
Kama sallaita 'ala 'Ibrahima
Wa 'ala 'ali 'Ibrahima,
'Inna-Ka Hamidun Majid
'Allahumma barik 'ala Muhammadin
Wa 'ala 'ali Muhammadin
Kama barakta 'ala 'Ibrahima
Wa 'ala 'ali 'Ibrahima,
'Inna-Ka Hamidun Majid"

(Translation)
O God, greetings upon Muhammad
and the family of Muhammad
as You greeted Abraham

and the family of Abraham,
Indeed! You are the Praiseworthy and Glorious One.
O God, bless Muhammad
and the family of Muhammad
as You blessed Abraham
and the family of Abraham,
Indeed! You are the Praiseworthy and Glorious One.

14. After saying these prayers, you turn your face to the right and say "As-salamu 'alaikum wa Rahmatullah" ("Peace and mercy of Allah be upon you") and then turn your face to the left and repeat the same words.

CONGRATULATIONS!

You've just completed two rak'ah of prayers! Not to confuse you, but each of the five daily required prayers has a different number of rak'ah or units that is customarily performed with each one. For a prayer that is longer than two rak'ah, only the "At-Tashahhud" is recited after the second rak'ah. Then you would repeat another rak'ah, reciting only "Surra al-Fatiha," then complete the rak'ah as instructed above. It sounds complicated, but isn't really that difficult, especially if you pray alongside someone who knows what they're doing. Check the Internet for a mosque near you, or call the closest university or college – there's sure to be a group of Muslims who get together to pray, especially on Fridays. (Friday is the day of congregational prayer in Islam.) Good luck!

Daily Prayer Schedule

Name	Time of Day	Number of Rak'ah
Fajr	Before sunrise	2
Zuhr	After 12:00PM	4
Asr	Mid-afternoon	4
Maghrib	Immediately after sunset	3
Isha	Night	4

Prayer Glossary

Fard – Obligatory, compulsory. This term refers to the five daily required prayers which entail the mandatory standing, bowing, and prostrating. 'Du'as' are basically prayers or supplications which can be uttered silently or aloud, in congregation or alone, at any time or place.

Niyah – Literally 'intention.' By reiterating your intention to pray before each prayer, you are reminding yourself that you are consciously performing an act of worship to and for God, not merely performing a ritual automatically as a robot.

Qiblah – The direction in which Muslims face while they say their prayers. Specifically, facing the direction of the Kaabah in Mecca, Saudi Arabia. Muslims do not worship the Kaabah. Rather, it represents a spiritual focus for prayer since Muslims revere the Kaabah as the first house of worship dedicated to the one God.

Sunnah – The actions of Prophet Muhammad. Since Muslims view Prophet Muhammad as the one person who embodies the highest levels of piousness and righteousness, they aspire to emulate his personal habits in an attempt to improve themselves and bring themselves closer to God. Prophet Muhammad often used to perform additional prayers after the fard prayers were completed. Thus, many Muslims also habitually perform these additional prayers, too.

Wudu – A ritual cleansing before prayer. Specifically, washing your hands, face, nose, mouth, head, ears, arms, and feet. This symbolically represents the spiritual cleansing that occurs when you pray. If water is unavailable, you can use clean sand or earth.

CHAPTER 4

Zakat

Charity: What Does It Mean?

> *"If you give alms openly, it is well;*
> *But if you do it secretly and give to the poor,*
> *that is better.*
> *This will absolve you of some of your sins;*
> *And God is cognisant of all you do."* [2:271]

In addition to faith and prayer, the Quran emphasizes the practice of doing good deeds. It's not enough to be a pious person in your head and live a life of excellent isolation - it's imperative to put your good intentions into practice and actually go out and DO GOOD. By translating good thoughts into good deeds, you 'walk the walk.' Sometimes it's boring and dull to always be good. (Aren't those the last words you always hear as you leave home?? "Be good!") Well, try doing good for a change – it's sometimes a challenge, but it's never dull or boring, and you may be surprised at all the good vibes you generate around you.

Islam emphasizes the importance of doing good deeds on a regular basis, which leads us to the topic of zakat (alms-giving or charity). Alms are anything given to relieve poverty or in order to help the poor. The concept of donating a portion of your savings or excess wealth on an annual basis is a sensible practice of welfare, especially in countries where the needy may not benefit from the existence of a welfare state. In addition, it's a small attempt to redistribute wealth in order to reduce the disparity between the 'haves' and the 'have nots.'

If a Muslim donates food, clothing, or money to the less fortunate around him, he is purifying his wealth in the sense that he can now enjoy his blessings with a clear conscience. By practicing charity on a regular basis, a Muslim can truly appreciate what God has given him while reminding himself that he may one day be in need of charity himself. This relationship between the rich and the poor is an important one because it serves as a reminder about the fleeting nature of material wealth in our lifetimes. The recommended amount to donate is 2.5% of your net worth, but whether you choose to donate more or less is between you and God.

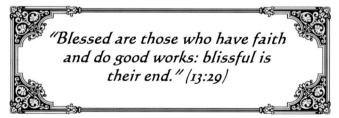

"Blessed are those who have faith and do good works: blissful is their end." (13:29)

A Teen's List of Charitable Ideas...

Action: Donate old clothes on a regular basis.
Reward: Your closet is less cluttered.

Action: Donate your favorite outfit instead of old stuff.
Reward: Imagine the look of happiness some lucky person will have!

Action: Turn over a week's allowance to your broke friend.
Reward: Maybe she'll do the same for you one day.

Action: Babysit for free.
Reward: The parents will be surprised and impressed.

Action: Treat the stranger behind you by paying his/her parking/admission
Reward: You'll put someone in a good mood for the rest of the day

Action: Drop $20 instead of $1 into the school fundraiser box.
Reward: The orphanage/homeless shelter/AIDS clinic needs it.

Action: Hand over your allowance to a homeless person.
Reward: You know you did a good deed, regardless of what they spend the money on.

Action: Fine-tune a skill/talent and use it to do good. For example, if you're in a band, play for free at a charity concert.
Reward: People get to enjoy your talent (maybe they'll hire you for a gig!)

39

The More You GIVE, the More You RECEIVE (Seriously!)

- Give a portion of your allowance to charity.

- Give freely of your smile

- Give generously around the house by cleaning up after yourself.

- Give up whining, complaining, and generally being a pain in the... neck.

- Give intellectual help to those in need (help your little brother with his homework!)

- Give a grateful word to your parents when they come home from work.

- Give up your Sunday afternoons to helping the elderly in your neighborhood with their chores, yardwork, etc.

- Receive – applause, appreciation, gratitude (ok – some disbelief, too!) from family, friends, and most importantly, from God.

CHAPTER 5

Relax - It's Ramadan
Tips For a Successful Fast

> *"Oh believers, fasting is enjoined on you*
> *As it was on those before you,*
> *So that you might become righteous."*
> *(2:183)*

What does 'enjoined' really mean? Have you ever wondered about that? According to Webster's Dictionary, 'enjoin' means "to direct or impose by authoritative order." Hmmm – that helps... a little. Ah, a secondary definition is "to lay down as a guide, direction, or rule of action, to designate or order the use of as a remedy." Now that makes more sense. God is commanding all the believers to fast, as their ancestors had done in the past, for their own good. Just as a prescription for medicine is intended to cure your illness, fasting is prescribed as medicine to cure... greed, lack of control, and by extension, teach spiritual fulfillment rather than physical fulfillment.

Think of fasting as shopping. You see this fantastic shirt at the mall but don't have enough cash to pay for it. When you finally get the shirt, you value it even more because you remember what you went through to get it. Fasting makes you feel grateful for having food on the table. Sometimes we take full stomachs (and full closets) for granted. Experiencing the pangs of hunger may encourage you to be more charitable to the homeless that sit on the sidewalk.

Muslims are asked to fast for the duration of the ninth month of the Islamic calendar – the month called 'Ramadan.' The Islamic calendar is based upon the new moon each month, which makes it about 11 days shorter than the Gregorian calendar that is in widespread use in America. What does that mean for Muslims? Basically that means that the month of Ramadan begins 11 days earlier each year. It's pretty easy to fast in the winter months when the days are short, but definitely a challenge in the summertime with long, hot days.

Does that mean that Muslims fast the entire month?? No. (There wouldn't be too many Muslims left standing if that were the case – no one could survive a month without any food or drink!) The fast is a daylight fast – Muslims fast from dawn to sunset each day. People who are traveling, ill, or unable to fast are exempted, as are children, pregnant women, and those who are nursing their babies. So God is not asking Muslims to fast as a punishment for their sins. Instead, fasting is seen as a physical and spiritual cleansing, as well as a test of will-power, fortitude, and determination. It recharges your spiritual battery! In addition, a successful fast requires not only giving up food and drink (yes, that includes water, gum, and cigarettes – a great time to give up smoking), but also the cessation of all bad habits such as gossiping, angry words due to impatience, laziness (sorry, but you can't use hunger as an excuse to get out of homework or cleaning your room!) etc. Try it – it's not that difficult once you put your mind to it.

Muslims all over the world enjoy the celebration called 'Eid al-Fitr' which is the festival at the end of the month of

Ramadan. Again, it is determined by the sighting of the new moon, which leads to much anticipation and excitement as the uncertainty caused by the sighting or lack of sighting leaves the Muslim community in suspense until the very last moment! Eid is a joyous day during which Muslims gather together in congregational prayer in the morning, usually in festive, new clothes, followed by visiting friends and family and enjoying a wonderful meal. Children traditionally receive gifts of money, clothes, and toys – so make sure you're in the social loop, as the definition of a 'child' can easily include young adults into their 30's! Let your neighbors know about your annual event by decorating your house with lights, garlands, and paper chains. Just because your house may not be festooned with red and green during Christmas doesn't mean that you don't enjoy your holidays! Share your traditions with your school – they'll appreciate learning something new about you. Even if your family came over on the Mayflower, you can share stories of how Muslims in different countries celebrate Eid. No matter how American you are, everyone loves a party!

Ramadan Do's and Dont's

Do eat a healthy, hearty, filling 'Suhoor/Sehri' (breakfast) before sunrise.

Do drink plenty of water, juice, water, coffee, water, and more water before you begin your fast!

Don't forget to wake up and EAT!!

Don't eat in front of other people who are fasting – it's impolite.

Don't forget to thank God for the delicious meal you enjoy at 'Iftar' (the meal you have at sunset) – some poor people may not even have that luxury.

Ramadan Recipes
[Very, very very easy!]

Cheesy Quesadillas
Quick and tasty
(and did we mention easy??)

Ingredients:

- 4 tortillas (corn or wheat)
- cheese (colby-jack/muenster is perfect) – thinly sliced or grated.
- salsa (don't make your own unless you're crazy... oops, I mean unless you really want to – the stuff out of the jar is pretty terrific, too.)
- chopped fresh or pickled jalapenos – yum!

Method:
Place cheese on a tortilla, top with salsa and jalapenos, then broil in toaster oven or microwave until cheese bubbles (hopefully not splatters all over the walls and ceiling of the microwave).

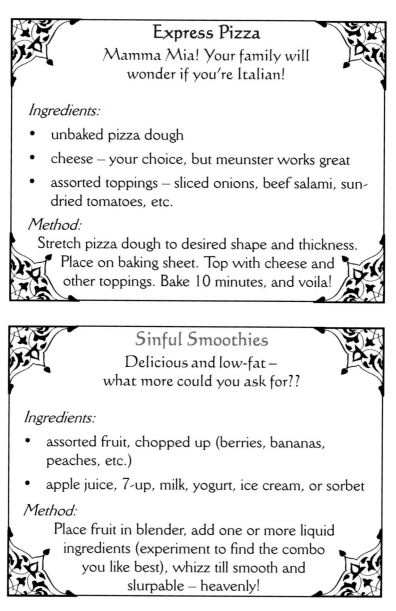

Express Pizza
Mamma Mia! Your family will
wonder if you're Italian!

Ingredients:

- unbaked pizza dough
- cheese – your choice, but meunster works great
- assorted toppings – sliced onions, beef salami, sun-dried tomatoes, etc.

Method:
Stretch pizza dough to desired shape and thickness. Place on baking sheet. Top with cheese and other toppings. Bake 10 minutes, and voila!

Sinful Smoothies
Delicious and low-fat –
what more could you ask for??

Ingredients:

- assorted fruit, chopped up (berries, bananas, peaches, etc.)
- apple juice, 7-up, milk, yogurt, ice cream, or sorbet

Method:
Place fruit in blender, add one or more liquid ingredients (experiment to find the combo you like best), whizz till smooth and slurpable – heavenly!

These recipes aren't specifically limited to Ramadan, so enjoy them whenever the mood strikes you – unleash the inner chef within!

Q and A

Q: Why is the month of Ramadan celebrated at different times every year?

A: Guess you skipped the beginning of this chapter. Muslims have an Islamic calendar that is based upon the moon. It's approximately 11 days shorter than the Gregorian calendar, which means all Islamic festivals move forward 11 days each year in relation to the Western calendar.

Q: Am I allowed to swallow spit, brush my teeth, or rinse my mouth while I'm fasting?

A: Please do! While some people feel strongly about these issues, you should use common sense as your guide. God knows what your intentions are, don't stress if you accidentally swallow some water while washing your face. Your friends and family will thank you for following some basic dental hygiene guidelines. In other words – **BRUSH!!**

Q: Do I have to break my fast with a date? (The fruit, not a boyfriend/girlfriend... we'll get to that topic later!)

A: It is customary for Muslims to break their fast by eating a date because that is how the Prophet Muhammad broke his fast. The instant sugar is easily digested and boosts the low blood sugar resulting from fasting. However, if you can't find a date or don't like them, eat whatever you like, you're celebrating completing your fast, not punishing yourself with boiled Brussels sprouts and liver!

Calling All Teens...
Do You Guys REALLY Fast?

M. Mannan (12), Texas: "Yes, every day of Ramadan. I started when I was 9."

Julia (12), Arizona: "Yes. Not a lot, but this year I'm going to try to fast for the whole month."

Esra (12), Illinois: "Sometimes. My mom thinks I'll get sick from not eating for a long time. I like fasting and want to do it. I began last year."

Anonymous (16): "Yes I do, but only on weekends because of school during the week."

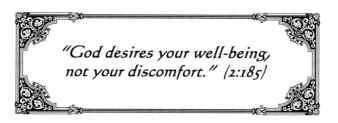

"God desires your well-being, not your discomfort." [2:185]

Celebrate Eid – Some Ideas...

- Decorate your house with lights.
- Decorate your hands with henna/mehndi.
- Buy presents for your friends and family (and drop hints about what you'd like!)
- Prepare festive dishes or splurge on a special meal in a fancy restaurant.
- Buy new clothes to wear to all the Eid parties and celebrations.
- Donate new clothes or food to the needy so that they can celebrate, too.
- Have a class party and share your holiday traditions with your school.
- Host an inter-faith gathering to discuss everyone's different holidays.
- Make Eid cards – when was the last time you used Elmer's glue and construction paper??
- Play upbeat, festive music from around the world to put you in the Eid mood.
- **HAVE FUN!!**

CHAPTER 6

Hajj
The Ultimate Road Trip

*"Announce the Pilgrimage to the people.
They will come to you on foot and riding along
distant roads
On lean and slender beasts,"* [22:27]

I magine millions of strangers gathered together shoulder to shoulder in one place for one common purpose. What could possibly unite them in such a mass gathering of single-minded devotion? The belief that they are following in the footsteps of Prophet Muhammad (who was himself following in the footsteps of the venerable Prophet Abraham and his son, Ishmael) in circumambulating the Kaabah and performing the sacred rites of the pilgrimage called 'Hajj.' The Hajj is the annual journey to visit the Kaabah in Mecca, Saudi Arabia. The pilgrimage takes place on the eighth, ninth, and tenth days of the twelfth month of the Islamic lunar calendar. Over 3 million Muslims gather each year to perform the Hajj, making it the single largest religious gathering anywhere in the world. In the words of Syed Aftab Azim's classic book on Hajj

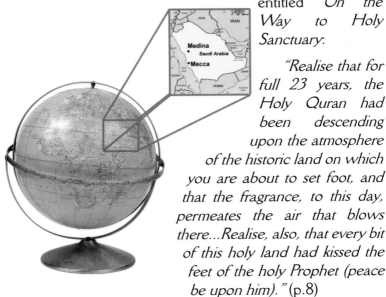

entitled *On the Way to Holy Sanctuary*.

"*Realise that for full 23 years, the Holy Quran had been descending upon the atmosphere of the historic land on which you are about to set foot, and that the fragrance, to this day, permeates the air that blows there...Realise, also, that every bit of this holy land had kissed the feet of the holy Prophet (peace be upon him).*" (p.8)

Most Muslims aspire to visit the Kaabah during the Hajj period, thus fulfilling their obligation to perform Hajj as it is stated in the Quran. However, if you are financially, physically, or otherwise unable to perform Hajj, you are excused from this ritual without incurring any penalty or being considered any less of a Muslim in the eyes of God. Just as a journey involves planning and preparation, performing the Hajj is as much a spiritual journey as it is a physical one. While some Muslims feel that they reached their spiritual peak whilst performing Hajj, others find deep satisfaction in going about their daily lives quietly fulfilling their Muslim duties as a way of life.

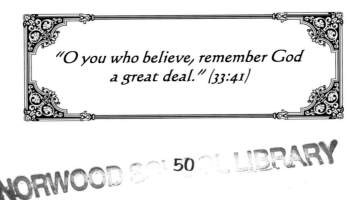

"*O you who believe, remember God a great deal.*" *[33:41]*

The Steps of Hajj — An Overview

1. Be a sane, adult Muslim who is physically and financially capable of the trip.

2. Wear 'Ihram' – two pieces of unstitched white cloth for men or modest dress for women which covers their head and body completely. (Wearing simple clothing emphasizes the spiritual equality of all the pilgrims – there is no distinction based upon fame, wealth, or power.)

3. 'Tawaf' – turning or circumambulation. Circle the Kaabah counterclockwise seven times.

4. 'Multazam' – prayer.

5. 'Maqam Ibrahim' (footprint of Prophet Abraham) – Recite blessing.

6. Well of Zamzam – drink the water from the well.

7. 'Sa'i' – brisk walk between the hills of Safa and Marwah.

8. 'Halq'/'Taqsir' – shave or cut off a piece of hair.

9. 'Mina' – stay in a tent for one day in the Mina Valley.

10. Plain of Arafat – remain for one day to commemorate Prophet Muhammad's Last Sermon.

11. 'Muzdalifah' – spend the night in open air at Muzdalifah.

12. Return to Mina – over the next three days, throw pebbles at 3 stone pillars representing the Devil.

13. Sacrifice – sacrifice a lamb or pay money for the sacrifice to be performed.

14. Bathe, change into everyday clothes, and perform final Tawaf in Mecca.

Don't let this step-by-step guide fool you. Hajj is not just a to-do list, but a journey filled with mystery and grandeur. Every Muslim who has ever completed a Hajj is at a loss for words to describe the multitude of emotions they felt during their stay in Mecca, Saudi Arabia. Michael Wolfe's *The Hadj* attempts to capture the magic of the experience in the following passage...

"One had to perform the tawaf to comprehend it. Its choreographic message, with God's house at the center, only came clear to me in the final rounds. Orbiting shoulder to shoulder with so many others induced in the end an open heart and a mobile point of view." (p.165)

Do You Anticipate Doing Hajj?

With over 150 responses to this one question - 99.4% of American Muslim teenagers answered with a resounding "Yes!" (Actually the responses varied from a lukewarm 'Kinda' to a more emphatic 'Yes, definitely', but they were all overwhelmingly in the affirmative.) Interesting, isn't it? Many teens may have difficulty performing the daily required prayers or annual fasts, but when it comes to their intention to visit Mecca and perform Hajj, they all feel the desire to worship at the Kaabah at least once in their lives.

Test Your Islamic IQ

(Relax – this test doesn't count. But it may help you on *Jeopardy* someday!)

1. The star and crescent are the symbols of Islam because...
   a) The cross was already taken.
   b) The star represents the guidance of Islam while the crescent moon illuminates the path of the believer through the darkness.
   c) It looks cool waving on a flag!

2. The Prophet Muhammad received the first revelation of the Quran in...
   a) The Cave of Wonders
   b) The Cave of Ali Baba (the 'Open Sesame' one)
   c) The Cave of Hira

3. The first surah revealed to the Prophet Muhammad was...
   a) Surah Iqra or Al-Alaq.
   b) Surah Fatihah (after all, it's the Opening of the Quran).
   c) Surah Al-Ikhlas (it's the first one I memorized!)

4. Which angel first spoke to the Prophet Muhammad?
    a) Angel Jibril (Gabriel)
    b) Angel of Mercy
    c) Angel on top of a Christmas tree

5. What is the Kaabah?
    a) The first house dedicated to the worship of one God
    b) The largest mosque in the world
    c) The study of Jewish mysticism

6. In which direction do you pray?
    a) North
    b) Towards the Kaabah
    c) To Disneyland

7. What is celebrated during Eid al-Adha?
    a) Prophet Abraham's willingness to obey God by sacrificing his son, Ishmael.
    b) The completion of the month of Ramadan.
    c) President George Washington's birthday.

8. How many pillars does Islam have?
    a) Zero – how can a religion have pillars?
    b) What do you mean, 'pillars?'
    c) 5

9. How often should you do Hajj?
    a) As often as you can – hey, who wouldn't want to vacation in a warm, sunny place?!
    b) Never – your grandfather already did it so your family is exempt.
    c) At least once in your life if you're physically and financially able.

10. When you perform Hajj, how many times do you circle the Kaabah?
   a) 7 – it's a lucky number.
   b) As many times as you can. After all, who knows when you'll return?!
   c) 7 – because that's how many times the Prophet Muhammad did.

Scoring:

1. a)2 b)3 c)1
2. a)2 b)1 c)3
3. a)3 b)2 c)1
4. a)3 b)2 c)1
5. a)3 b)1 c)2

6. a)2 b)3 c)1
7. a)3 b)2 c)1
8. a)2 b)1 c)3
9. a)1 b)2 c)3
10. a)2 b)1 c)3

What's It All Mean??

24 points or more – Congratulations! You're a proud, confident, knowledgable teen. Great job! Don't neglect the other aspects of Islam, though – being a Muslim is more than just knowing Islamic history.

15-23 points – Good work, but you still have some learning to do.

Less than 15 points – Where have you been? Turn off the TV and run, don't walk, to your nearest Islamic School for some serious studying!

NOTES

CHAPTER 7

The Quran

Islam's Holy Book

> *"This Qur'an is not such (a writ) as*
> *could be composed*
> *By anyone but God.*
> *It confirms what has been revealed before,*
> *And is an exposition of (Heaven's) law.*
> *Without any doubt it's from the Lord of all*
> *the worlds." (10:37)*

The Quran (Koran) is the holy book for Muslims, just
as the Torah is for Jews and the Bible is for Christians.
Muslims believe it was revealed to Prophet Muhammad by
Angel Gibrail (Gabriel) over a period of 23 years, beginning in
610 AD. It literally means 'The Recitation' as it was revealed
orally. Verses were written down and memorized as they
were revealed, but it was only in 650 AD that all the various
copies were collected, compared, and then the most accurate
one was preserved whilst the others were destroyed. In this
manner, the original Quran has been preserved in Arabic up
to this day – with not one word altered in over 1,400 years!

Of course, not all Muslims read Arabic, so the Quran is widely available in translations in over 40 different languages today.

There are 114 suras or chapters in the Quran, ranging in length from a few lines to almost 40 pages. They cover a variety of topics from the creation of the world, heaven and hell, and the day of judgment, to legal issues such as marriage, divorce, inheritance, and the rights of orphans, to fables and stories of prophets familiar to Jews and Christians including Adam and Eve, Noah, and Moses. The chapters are arranged in order of length, with the longest ones at the beginning and the shortest ones at the end. Sura Fatihah is the exception to this rule as it is known as 'The Opening' and is always the first sura in a Quran. In addition to this method of arrangement, most Qurans will also identify where the chapter was revealed, i.e., Mecca or Medina. This distinction is helpful in fully understanding the chapter by giving the historical time-frame and place – many suras were revealed in order to show the Prophet the correct course of action or to guide the community of growing Muslims in their quest for a righteous life in the worship of God.

Why is it important for Muslims to read the Quran? After all, it seems confusing, repetitive, and disjointed to the average reader who tries to read it from cover to cover as a novel or a regular book. But that's the problem – the Quran isn't just a 'regular book.' However, if you view it as the holy word of God that contains instructions on how to lead a good life in order to reach Heaven in the after-life, then simply pick up a copy, open it at random, or better yet, begin at the ending and read the short, early Meccan chapters first. You'll be amazed at the rhythm, beauty, and rhyme of the language of the Quran and the eloquence and simplicity of its message will mesmerize you. The pursuit of knowledge is a requirement for all of mankind, and most especially for Muslims, for the first word revealed to Prophet Muhammad was...

"Read!" 96:1

True or False??

1. Every Muslim has to memorize the Quran.

Trick statement. The answer is both true and false. Most Muslims memorize at least 2 suras (chapters), especially the first one, which is called Al-Fatihah (The Opening or The Beginning). It's an essential part of the required prayer and encapsulates the entire message of the Quran in its simplicity and beauty. Then most Muslims would also memorize another

short sura as the daily prayer requires the recitation of 2 suras. Many people never memorize more than 2 or 3 short suras, while others memorize the entire Quran and earn the honorific title 'Hafiz' – which means one who has memorized the Quran.'

2. I have to be clean before I touch the Quran.

Another trick statement. True, in the sense that you should treat the Quran with respect and never place it on the floor, put your feet on it, or intentionally destroy it. Most scholars would require the state of cleanliness which is required for the 5 daily prayers before approaching the Quran. Ensure that your hands are clean and approach it at all times as a source of knowledge and guidance.

It is false, in the sense that while some cultural traditions require that both men and women must be in a state of the utmost cleanliness and purity before touching the Quran, this approach would rule out many men and women who turn to the Quran on a daily basis, but who may not be in a state of 'wudu' or the level of purity required for prayer. Use your common sense and try and be as clean as possible.

3. It only counts if you read the Quran in Arabic.

Absolutely false! Knowledge is knowledge, regardless of what language it's in. God made humanity in different colors with different languages so that we could learn from each other and appreciate as well as overcome our differences. Whilst the original Arabic may contain beauty and poetry that can only be truly appreciated by a native Arabic speaker, there are numerous translations of great eloquence. Browse through a few different translations at your bookstore and select the one that resonates within you. While many scholars would argue in favor of reading the Quran only in Arabic, in this instance, follow the route which brings you closer to God, whether through literal understanding or spiritual transcendence.

4. I don't need to read the Quran. My mother/father/ older brother/sister/cousin/uncle/etc. already told me everything I need to know about it.

False. That's great that your relatives are so willing to share their knowledge with you, but that doesn't excuse you from reading it yourself! The only way to form an unbiased understanding of the Quran is to pick it up and read it for yourself. Discuss it all you want with whomever you choose, but definitely read it with you own eyes and think about it with your own brain. Don't rely exclusively on someone else's explanations, no matter how well meaning or wise they are. Form your own opinion.

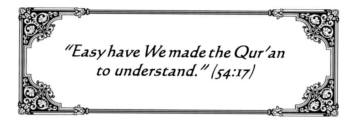

"Easy have We made the Qur'an to understand." (54:17)

F.Y.I.

- The earliest complete copies of the Quran date from the 9th century, although fragments of older Qurans do exist, some as old as the 7th century.

- The Quran as we know it today dates back to the collection of verses that Hafsa, one of the Prophet's wives, had in her possession and which she made available to Othman, the 3rd Caliph. After comparing her collection to the recitation of several people who had memorized the Quran, he was able to compile a single, accurate version of the Quran which is the version that Muslims all over the world read.

Teen Tips for Reading the Quran

- Find a paperback translation which you like and will actually read!

- Keep it in your backpack or on your bedside table so it's always handy.

- Treat yourself to a nice bookmark and use it so that you don't lose your place and have to perpetually reread the hard parts!

- Talk about what you've read with your friends and family.

- Make up your own 'Quran Summer Reading Program,' and reward yourself frequently and generously!

- Get your parents to promise that they'll throw a huge party in your honor if you actually finish it, and then read your little heart out!

- Ask for help if you don't understand what you're reading – it's not always clear.

- Don't ever give up. It's okay if it takes you years to finish reading the Quran – it's still a huge achievement.

CHAPTER 8

Prophet Muhammad

A Short Version of a Long Story

"You are only a bearer of warnings.
We have sent you with the truth,
To give glad tidings and to warn.
Never has there been a community
To which an admonisher was not sent." (35:23-24)

The Prophet Muhammad was born in 570 AD in Mecca, Saudi Arabia. His father, Abdullah, died before Muhammad was born, and his mother, Aminah, passed away when he was only six. He lived with his paternal grandfather, Abd al-Muttalib, until the age of eight when, sadly, his grandfather too passed away. Muhammad's uncle, Abu Talib, became his guardian and raised him as if he were his own son. Although Muhammad suffered many losses during his childhood, he grew up to be a polite, respectful, and truthful young man.

Muslims believe that there were many signs that intimated at Muhammad's future role as a Messenger of God. For example, it was the custom in Arabia for parents to allow foster mothers to care for their young children in the desert villages far from the pollution and crowding of the cities. When Halimah, a poor woman with few resources of her own, took charge of the baby Muhammad, her farm animals miraculously began giving plentiful milk for the whole family. The drought which had been plaguing her village ended, and the crops grew rapidly and abundantly. While Muhammad was a young boy, he met a Christian monk named Buhaira who recognized in Muhammad several signs that the boy was especially blessed by God. Buhaira predicted that Muhammad would have a great future and advised Abu Talib to watch over him carefully.

Muhammad grew to manhood and became a businessman. He oversaw caravans that would carry goods for trade between cities throughout Arabia. After proving his trust-worthiness and business acumen, his employer Khadijah, a wealthy widow, asked for his hand in marriage. He accepted and enjoyed 25 years of happily married life with her. It was only in 610 AD, at the age of 40, that Muhammad began receiving revelations from God through the Angel Gabriel. These revelations continued until the Prophet's death in Medina in 632 AD. The Prophet was only 62 when he passed away.

Muslims all over the world respect and revere the Prophet as the last Messenger, an example of the ideal Muslim, and most of all, as the recipient of the Quran. The Quran emphasizes the fact that Muhammad was a man, not the son of God. His fallibility was a sign that no one is perfect – an important concept in Islam that ensures that while Muslims accept their limitations, they can also strive to follow the example of the Prophet. In addition to the Quran, Muslims try to learn as much as possible about the life and sayings of the Prophet in order to model their life after that of the Prophet's. The sayings of the Prophet are called 'hadiths'. Approximately 150 years after his death, several notable scholars compiled collections of hadiths after meticulously evaluating each saying for its veracity and chain of transmission. The actions during the life of Muhammad are called his 'sunnah', and many Muslims try to emulate the Prophet by leading their lives in a similar manner to his.

A widespread misconception amongst non-Muslims is the belief that Muslims worship the Prophet Muhammad. Nothing could be farther from the truth! Muslims traditionally bow before no man. There are countless stories of Muslim travelers visiting foreign potentates and politely excusing themselves from bowing by explaining that in Islam, man bows only before God or whilst in prayer to God. While Muslims revere and respect all the prophets beginning with Adam and ending with Muhammad, they are usually more knowledgeable about the Prophet Muhammad in particular because many details from his life have been recorded for posterity as he was the most recent prophet.

Who Was Prophet Muhammad?

1. *Prophet Muhammad was a businessman.*
   He successfully led trading caravans across the desert.

2. *Prophet Muhammad was a Messenger of God.*
   He received the Quran from God as a message for mankind for all time.

3. *Prophet Muhammad was a husband.*
   His first marriage to Khadijah lasted for 25 years. His subsequent marriages were contracted for several reasons – treaties with feuding tribes, removing the stigma of marrying widows or divorcees or former slaves, demonstrating marriage as acceptable with 'People of the Book' (Jews and Christians), etc.

4. *Prophet Muhammad was a leader.*
   He created a community of Muslims in Medina with laws, rules, and charitable customs.

5. *Prophet Muhammad was the Seal of the Prophets.*
   Muslims believe that Muhammad was the last Prophet to be sent by God—'sealing' the last position in the historic line of Prophets.

6. *Prophet Muhammad was a man.*
   He was a man, not the son of God. As such, he was human and faced all the temptations and limitations any other man would face. However, as one of God's chosen ones, Muhammad was blessed with faith in God.

7. *Prophet Muhammad was a father.*
   He had three sons and four daughters, but unfortunately all of his sons died in infancy, and all of his daughters except Fatima died before him.

True or False??

1. The Prophet married more than four wives at a time, so all Muslims can, too.

Trick question – true in that the Prophet did marry more than four wives at a time due to the examples of permissible marriageable partners which he was trying to set, but false in that God states quite clearly in the Quran that no other man should take more than four wives, and actually shouldn't marry more than once if he fears that he will be unable to treat his wives fairly and equally.

2. The Prophet Muhammad taught us how to pray.

True – God repeatedly asks us in the Quran to pray, but the specific postures and words are not stated definitively. The customary manner in which Muslims worldwide pray has been adopted since the lifetime of Prophet Muhammad as people emulated his form of worship.

3. The leader of the Muslim community has to be a descendant of the Prophet.

Another trick question. After the Prophet passed away, Abu Bakr, a respected Muslim who was the Prophet's close friend and father-in-law, was chosen to lead the Muslim community. However, a group of Muslims felt that the Prophet's cousin and son-in-law, Ali, should have been the rightful leader as the closest descendant of the Prophet. This disagreement in succession has led to the primary division in the Muslim world – Sunnis accept Abu Bakr and the subsequent caliphs as rightful leaders, whilst the Shias recognize only Ali (the fourth caliph) and the descendants of Ali as rightful leaders. Approximately 90% of Muslims are Sunnis and 10% are Shias.

4. Hadiths and sunnah are as important as the Quran.

False – Hadiths (sayings) and the sunnah (examples) of Prophet Muhammad are important to Muslims as they explain and elaborate on specifics, but nothing that contradicts the Quran is permissible. The Quran remains the ultimate authority and guide for Muslims, whilst the hadiths and sunnah are useful as secondary sources and aides to more fully understanding the Quran and the body of Islamic jurisprudence which has developed over the ages.

How Well Do You Know Your Prophets?

1. Eve's husband was
   a) Moses
   b) Abraham
   c) Adam
   d) Muhammad

2. Which prophet built an ark upon God's instruction?
   a) David
   b) Noah
   c) Joseph
   d) Jonah

3. The first female prophet was
   a) Eve
   b) Mary
   c) The Queen of Sheba
   d) none of the above

4. Which two prophets rebuilt the Kaabah?
   a) Castor and Pollux
   b) Tweedledee and Tweedledum
   c) David and Goliath
   d) Abraham and Ishmael

5. Which prophet received the Torah from God?
   a) Moses
   b) Jesus
   c) Abraham
   d) Muhammad

6. Which prophet was blessed with extraordinary wisdom?
   a) Job
   b) Solomon
   c) Noah
   d) Aaron

7. Which prophet parted the Red Sea? (Hint: think 'Prince of Egypt.')
   a) David
   b) Jesus
   c) Moses
   d) Pharaoh

8. Which prophet suffered many hardships but never lost his faith in God?
   a) Adam
   b) Noah
   c) Abraham
   d) Job

Answers:

1. c – Adam

2. b – Noah

3. d – None of the above, even though Mary, the Queen of Sheba, and Moses's mother are mentioned several times in the Quran as pious women who deserve respect and praise.

4. d – Abraham and Ishmael

5. a – Moses

6. b – Solomon

7. c – Moses

8. d – Job

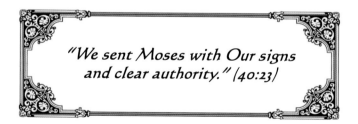

"We sent Moses with Our signs and clear authority." [40:23]

25 Prophets Mentioned in The Quran

Arabic Name	Biblical Name	Arabic Name	Biblical Name
Adam	Adam	Musa	Moses
Idris	Enoch	Harun	Aaron
Nuh	Noah	Dhul-kifl	Ezekiel
Hud	(none)	Dawud	David
Salih	Salih	Sulaiman	Solomon
Ibrahim	Abraham	Ilyas	Elias
Ismail	Ishmael	Al-Yasa	Elisha
Ishaq	Isaac	Yunus	Jonah
Lut	Lot	Zakkariya	Zachariah
Yaqub	Jacob	Yahya	John
Yusuf	Joseph	Isa	Jesus
Shuaib	(none)	Muhammad	(none)
Ayyub	Job		

NOTES

CHAPTER 9

Halal and Haram
Can I Go to McDonald's?

> *"O believers, eat what is good of the food*
> *We have given you, and be grateful to God,*
> *If indeed you are obedient to Him.*
> *Forbidden to you are carrion and blood,*
> *And the flesh of the swine,*
> *And that which has been*
> *Consecrated (or killed)*
> *In the name of any other than God."*
> *(2:172-173)*

Halal and haram – you've heard the words before, but were never sure exactly what they meant, right? Basically, everything is allowed or 'halal' except that which is expressly forbidden or 'haram.' So according to a loose interpretation of the above verses, when it comes to food, Muslims can eat freely of all the food around them except for dead meat (also known as carrion—rotting meat unfit for human consumption), blood (needs no explanation), swine (pork, ham, bacon etc.), and anything that has been slaughtered in the name of anyone other than God.

The first three categories are clear and simple to follow – pass on the road-kill and order your burger minus the bacon. It's the last instruction that gives rise to confusion. A strict interpretation requires meat to be slaughtered in a certain humane manner in which the throat of the animal is slit and the blood is allowed to drain from the carcass. In addition, the animal must be slaughtered in the name of God and a prayer must be recited by the butcher in order for the meat to be deemed halal or kosher.

So where does that leave McDonald's? Strictly speaking, the beef or chicken is not halal because it was not slaughtered in the customary Islamic manner. However, it was not slaughtered in the name of any other God either. In fact, it was not slaughtered in anyone's name. Since many Muslims are accustomed to uttering a short prayer or simply saying 'Bismillah' (in the name of God) before they begin eating, the widely held view is that this custom confers a halal blessing on the food. By thanking God for the food they are about to eat, Muslims remember God, thank him for his blessings, and thus render the food halal in their estimation. The Quran also contains the following verse in regard to food:

"Eat only that over which the name of God Has been pronounced, if you truly believe in His commands." [6:118]

Therefore some Muslims residing in America, for example, are comfortable with saying 'Bismillah' before meals, and then eating beef, lamb, or chicken in restaurants and cafeterias, confident that they are following God's instructions in spirit, if not in the letter of the law.

Haram refers to the category of food and activities which are expressly forbidden in Islam. In addition to the guidelines for food, haram activities include drinking alcohol, indulging in drugs, and gambling. At first glance, it's obvious why these practices are to be avoided. Drinking can lead to a state of intoxication which can lead to loss of control of oneself or a car, for example. Taking drugs is harmful, self-destructive, and can expose you to the dangers of AIDS or even death. Gambling is a waste of one's money. Plus, all these activities are illegal anyway for anyone under the age of 21, so that definitely rules out all the teenagers reading this book! Any of these activities done in excess can lead to depression, poverty, or even suicide. So be smart and say 'No' when invited to partake in these haram situations.

Although the initial reference to these activities in the Quran (2:219) says that there is pleasure as well as harm in these things and simply denounces them rather than forbidding them outright, later references (5:90-91) instruct Muslims to avoid them altogether as they can lead one to forget God and go far astray. After all, our society wouldn't have a need for AA

(Alcoholics Anonymous), GA (Gamblers Anonymous), or NA (Narcotics Anonymous) if it wasn't such a crisis. The numerous substance-abuse rehab programs that are available all over the country highlight the huge problem that is currently facing America — too many people are

addicted to these harmful habits which not only ruin their own lives but the lives of countless other friends and relatives as well. Taking a serious look at these issues emphasizes the wisdom of the Quran when it counsels Muslims to avoid these activities.

Any college-bound teenager in America realizes the temptations to be faced in the years ahead. Rather than isolating yourself in your room or the library, you'll find that it is possible to fully enjoy the college experience (including attending sporting events, study groups, and parties) without engaging in any haram activities. Many non-Muslim teenagers have first-hand knowledge of the destructive effects of drinking and driving, or experimenting with drugs in high school. College students are usually older and wiser than high-schoolers (well, ok – that may be an overly optimistic statement!); this maturity should translate itself into better decision-making skills in college. So find some like-minded friends and be true to your beliefs. Peer pressure is only pressure when you are insecure or unsure of yourself. When in doubt, do the right thing. Remember, while you may fool yourself, your roommate, and your parents, you're never fooling God.

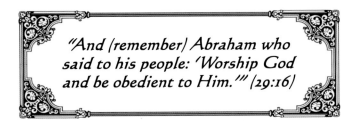

"And [remember] Abraham who said to his people: 'Worship God and be obedient to Him.'" [29:16]

Halal or Haram – You Decide...

1. Going trick or treating – halal or haram?

2. Drinking flat beer (after all, it's not fizzy anymore...)?

3. Eating a BLT (bacon, lettuce, and tomato) sandwich made with turkey bacon?

4. Drinking root beer?

5. Eating a hot dog?

6. Eating Chinese food?

7. Oreos, marshmallows, and Krispy Kreme doughnuts?

8. Pepperoni Pizza?

Answers:

1. Halal – What's wrong with some free candy? God never outlawed candy.

2. Haram – Beer is beer, so avoid it. It tastes terrible, is full of calories, and will make you fat and drunk if you drink too much.

3. Halal – Turkey bacon is perfectly acceptable. Bon appetit!

4. Halal – Root beer is non-alcoholic. Go ahead and chug away!

5. Depends on what it's made of – Check the label. If it's all-beef, turkey, or chicken, then you're good to go. Pass on it if you're in doubt or can't tell.

6. Halal – Chinese food is delicious. Just make sure your food doesn't have any pork or ham, especially in the soups.

7. Check the labels – Some doughnuts are fried in lard (pork fat), but Krispy Kremes aren't, so get 'em while they're hot! Some cookies contain gelatin which may be derived from pigs. Read the labels and use your own judgment.

8. Haram while it has pepperoni on it – Sorry. Stick with cheese or vegetarian pizza to be on the safe side, or check to see if the pepperoni is made from beef or turkey.

I Feel Alone When...

- My best friend is talking about her date this weekend.
- Everybody is going Christmas shopping.
- I'm the only one picking the pepperoni off the pizza.
- Everybody is talking about the wild party last night (the one I wasn't allowed to go to).
- I don't know all the words to a Christmas carol.
- Sometimes I have to say 'No' when I want to say 'Yes.'
- I want to say my prayers, but I don't want my friends to think I'm weird.
- I wish I had the courage to SPEAK OUT, but I keep quiet instead.

I'm Not So Alone When...

- I'm celebrating Ramadan iftars with my family and friends.
- Everybody is buying new clothes for Eid.
- I get to eat whatever I want for sehri (even spaghetti or ice cream at 5am!)
- Everyone is enjoying the Eid parties and celebrations.
- I know all the words to 'The Star-Spangled Banner' (and even the tune).
- Sometimes I have to say 'No' when I want to say 'Yes,' but my friends are in the same boat, too.
- I'm surrounded by Muslims at Eid prayers, all bowing and praying together.
- I SPEAK OUT and sometimes people listen.

NOTES

CHAPTER 10

The 4 'D's
Dating, Dancing, Drinking, and Drugs

> *"They ask you concerning wine and gambling.*
> *Say, 'In them is great sin, and some profit,*
> *for men;*
> *But the sin is greater than the profit.'"*
> *(2:219 - Yousef Ali)*

Did you turn to this chapter first? If you're hoping to find that Islam gives you permission to freely indulge in all of the above...sorry to disappoint you. Islam does forbid drinking and gambling (see Chapter 9 for a more thorough discussion of halal and haram.) The Quran initially refers somewhat ambivalently to drinking and gambling, as noted in the verse cited above, but it later forbids both habits outright (5:90-91). Basically, Islam takes the viewpoint that anything which intoxicates or interferes with rational thought is forbidden.

Therefore, drinking, drugs, and by extension, gambling, are all considered harmful and should be avoided at all costs. All of these activities can contribute to the breakdown of the family unit, the dissolution of strong communities, and the downfall of many strong characters who somehow thought addiction could never happen to them.

Does listening to music fall into the same category? Well, depends on the person, the music, and the interpretation. If listening to rock or hip-hop puts you into a good mood, then go right ahead. But if listening to violent lyrics or suicidal dirges depresses you, then switch over to a more upbeat station – use your common sense! Don't let music, or for that matter, any one habit obsess you. Keep your perspective – listen to music if you like, but don't let it take over your life. Sure, your parents will probably yell at you to turn it down, so humor them. If you maintain a good balance in your life by putting school first and proving to them that you have goals, they'll be more likely to indulge your growing CD collection. Will listening to music automatically disqualify you from getting into Heaven? Of course not, but you have to use your head and moderate your listening. Does music lead to dancing? Dancing with members of the opposite sex? Is all this haram? Yes and no. There aren't many easy answers when it comes to these gray areas. Dancing in all male/all female environments is definitely okay, (although it may not be the norm in high school), while dancing with members of the opposite sex is frowned upon if it leads to physical contact or suggestive moves. On this topic, you'll have to consult your parents on their views and respect their wishes. Ask them to explain their stance – if you give them a chance to explain their experiences as teens, it may help you understand their point of view and vice versa.

Dating can be another taboo topic. Most parents take the easy way out and just forbid it. But what does the Quran really say on the topic? Unfortunately, the references don't deal specifically with this issue. Men and women are equal in the eyes of God, and they should both respect each other. Marriage is stressed for many reasons. Among them are the alleviating of sexual desires in the sanctity of marriage, the legal responsibility of the husband to care for any children born to his wife, and the general happiness of the community. Given that it's natural for you to want to meet your spouse before marriage in order to make sure that you'll be happy, how can you achieve this without dating?

If your parents had an arranged marriage and expect the same of you, you need to sit down and frankly discuss your expectations with them, especially if they differ from your parents'. It's not always easy growing up in the American teen culture which places so much emphasis on dating in high school, but determine what's right for you and your family. Setting ground rules will help. Communication is key to a happy high school experience with your parents. If you lie to them even once and they find out, you'll have to build up their trust in you all over again – it could take months! So be open and honest and let them know how you feel. Dating should only be viewed as a preliminary step to marriage. If you're not ready for marriage, then don't date. It's truly as simple as that. Go out with your friends in a group – you'll have fun and won't get bogged down emotionally with a lot of feelings that you're not ready for as a teen. Concentrate on your academics, sports, and volunteer activities while some of your friends are getting side-tracked with boyfriends and girlfriends. You'll be ahead in the long run.

Help – I want to date, but my parents won't let me!

1. *Does Islam forbid dating?*
   In the sense that it could lead to pre-marital sex, then yes. But the Quran specifically states that a woman must agree to a marriage, which implies that she can get to know her future husband in order to decide - how chaperoned the setting should be can depend on your culture and your parents' preferences.

2. *My friends will think I'm a loser if I don't date.*
   Hey, you won't have to deal with all the boyfriend/ girlfriend drama! Be true to yourself, but don't argue or try to convince them. Tell them that you're waiting for the right person to come along...

3. *How can I convince my parents to let me date?*

Examine your motives - do you truly want to get to know someone better, or do you just want to go out with your friends? Be honest with your parents and respect their views. Maybe they trust you, but aren't sure of your date. Intentions are as important as actions in this case, so err on the right side by not putting yourself into a situation which you'll regret. If you just want to hang out with your friends occasionally, tell your parents and find a middle ground which you can both accept.

4. *Is dating allowed if I stick to other Muslims?*

Well, you're on the right track in the sense that you could potentially marry this person with little religious objections from your family. Dating between Muslims should theoretically be allowed as both parties will be aware of the physical limits implied in the Quran. As long as your parents are aware that you're not doing anything wrong and your intentions are to get to know each other better with the ultimate goal of marriage in mind, then go right ahead (but please confirm that it's ok with your parents!)

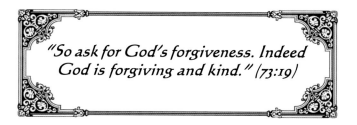

"So ask for God's forgiveness. Indeed God is forgiving and kind." (73:19)

What Are Teens Saying??

100% of American Muslim teens will avoid drugs – smart thinking!

100% of American Muslim teens will avoid drinking – it's unIslamic and uncool.

80% of American Muslim teens think dating as teens is dumb:

- *Yasmine* (13), Arizona: "You're not going to marry the person now, so what's the point?"

70% of American Muslim teens think dancing is ok, but only with members of the same sex – better to be safe than sorry. Slow dancing could lead to arousal which could lead to... unwanted consequences.

- *Amira* (16), Ohio: "Doing or participating in one leads to the others."

- *Naaz* (15), Illinois: "All of them are wrong and are influenced by the American culture and media."

- *Maymuna* (11), Texas: "I think people are weird to even try them. Dating, drinking, and drugs are dumb to try, but dancing is ok.

Random Thoughts About Why I Love Being a Muslim

- I get presents of money during Eid.

- Since Eid occurs twice a year, I get money twice!

- I can talk directly to God when I pray (no intermediary priests or bishops).

- I'm helping the pigs stay alive by not eating them.

- The star and crescent are beautiful symbols associated with Islam.

- I've heard alcohol tastes terrible, so I'm glad that I can't drink it.

- I have fun being a Muslim!

- I don't have to eat dry matzo crackers or dry fruitcake after religious holidays. (OK, I do have to help finish off all the dry dates left over after Ramadan.)

NOTES

CHAPTER 11

Misunderstandings & Misconceptions
Are All Muslims Terrorists??

"Whatever is in the heavens and the earth sings the praises of God. He is All-mighty and All-wise." (59:1)

Islam is the fastest growing religion in America, but remains one of the most misunderstood. Becoming knowledgable about Islam is the first step in educating others about your beliefs, but in order to truly have an intelligible discussion about Muslim issues, you also have to be acquainted with others' faiths and beliefs as well. Patiently explaining some of the main similarities between your religion and another's religion is important, but seeing friends and strangers have that "Oh, I never knew you believed in the

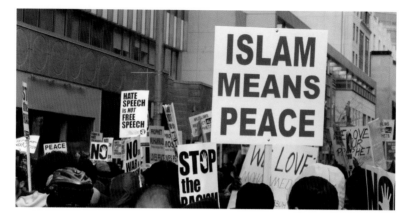

same God I do" moment is priceless! As the global community of mankind continues to shrink (thanks to the instantaneous sharing of information and ideas on the Internet), it behooves all of us to become familiar with other religions and cultures in order to reduce misunderstandings. There's a fine line between ignorance and racism – confrontations are more likely to arise between strangers who mistrust each other's 'differences' than between strangers who are informed and educated.

So where does that leave American Muslim teens? Whether it's in school or in the workplace, you're sure to come across people who are surprised/bored/scared by your religious identity. Put them at their ease by answering their questions honestly and openly. It's better to say "I don't know" if you're asked about a topic you're not familiar with than to make up an answer which could cause more confusion down the road!

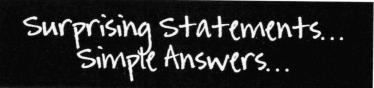

Surprising Statements...
Simple Answers...

1. Muslims worship a different God than Jews & Christians.

No, actually Muslims believe in the one God, the God of Abraham and Jesus, the same God most people refer to when they say 'God.' American Muslims may only have themselves to blame for this misunderstanding as most of them customarily refer to God as 'Allah,' (the word for God in Arabic). Amongst English-speakers, it may be preferable to just say 'God' rather than 'Allah' as it will reduce the confusion which arises when strangers insist, "You worship Allah while I worship God – see, I knew you worship a different God!"

2. All Muslims speak Arabic.

Again, the answer is 'No,' even though most Muslims are familiar with common phrases such as the Arabic greeting of 'Salaam alleikum,' which means 'Peace be upon you,' and short prayers/religious utterances such as 'Bismillah,' which means 'In the name of God.' There's no requirement that you have to speak Arabic in order to be a Muslim.

3. Islam is a religion that mistreats/demeans women.

Definitely not – in fact, Islam is a surprisingly enlightened religion when compared to many other faiths, especially taking into account the traditional sixth century Arab society in which Islam first

91

appeared. Women have the right to own and inherit property, vote, and seek gainful employment under the guidelines clearly stated in the Quran. Discrimination against women, or indeed against anyone based upon race, religion, or ethnicity goes against the principles of Islam. While most countries attempt to treat men and women equally, in reality, women are as likely to earn less than men, for example, in a non-Muslim country as they are in a Muslim one. Religion really has very little to do with discrimination per se; discrimination usually stems from ignorance, cultural traditions, or economic hardship.

4. Only Muslims go to Heaven.

The Quran specifically states that all believers will be rewarded with Paradise, and it also states that only God can judge mankind, therefore it's futile to speculate who will and won't end up in Heaven. (98:7-8) According to Muslim beliefs, God is interested in pious, righteous people who do good deeds on this Earth - so if you give much thought to the afterlife and are worried about where you may end up, do as many good deeds as possible!

5. All Muslims are terrorists!

Sadly, after the attacks of 9/11, some people actually blamed an entire religion for the murderous acts of a few fanatics. It's morally wrong and intellectually reprehensible to blame an entire group for the actions of a few, so assuming that you're dealing with a rational person who confronts you with the above viewpoint, you should be able to calmly state that Islam does not encourage or condone terrorism. In the Quran, taking another's life is compared to killing all of humanity. Murdering innocent civilians is forbidden in any religion.

While American Muslims endured heightened scrutiny and faced unwarranted suspicion in post-9/11 America, they also appreciated the benefits which came about through the education of the general public about Islam. Suspicions gradually subsided as individual Muslims went about their daily lives as peaceful citizens of this country, proving to their friends, neighbors, and colleagues that the hijackers definitely did not speak for the vast majority of Muslims around the world. The history of America is one of immigrants pursing their dreams in a land where freedom of speech, press, and religion are all highly prized values. The Muslim immigrant experience has been challenged by 9/11, but this generation will be stronger and more integrated into the fabric of American society if they rise to the challenge of explaining that their faith should not be blamed for the extremist actions of a few men. The responsibility to educate ourselves as well as each other lies within each of us. Whether we welcome this opportunity or avoid it at all costs may determine the happiness of successive generations of American Muslims.

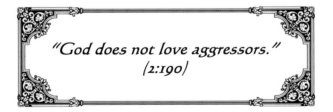

"God does not love aggressors."
[2:190]

93

NOTES

CHAPTER 12

The Hijab Issue
Unveil the Controversy

> *"O Prophet, tell your wives and daughters*
> *And the women of the faithful,*
> *To draw their wraps a little over them.*
> *They will thus be recognised and no harm will*
> *come to them.*
> *God is forgiving and kind." (33:59)*

Perhaps no other single issue in Islam has generated more discussion amongst women than the issue of hijab. Covering one's hair has become an identifying badge of one's 'Muslimness' – regardless of the intentions behind the decision. While only God truly knows what is in our hearts, many Muslim girls and women are wearing head-scarves for a multitude of different reasons. Hijab literally means 'a partition' or 'a separation.' Among Muslims, the term 'hijab' has come to mean covering one's hair and fully covering one's body, leaving only the face and hands visible. What does the

Quran say about hijab? Interestingly, nowhere in the Quran does it emphatically state that women must cover their hair. Both believing men and women are instructed to dress modestly and not display themselves showily or unnecessarily to others. In addition, women are instructed to cover their bosoms and not walk in such a way as to draw attention to the swaying of their bodies. So according to the Quran, as long as Muslims are dressed modestly and behave respectably, no specific dress code is required. As an adjunct to modest dress, modest behavior is also encouraged, therefore ogling the cute boy in Chemistry class or leering at the cheerleaders is definitely out! Needless to say, each person must read the Quran for herself and form her own opinion.

The controversy over hijab arises from a hadith (saying of the Prophet Muhammad) repeated by Aisha, one of the Prophet's wives as follows:

> "A'isha said: 'Asma', daughter of Abu Bakr, entered upon the Apostle of Allah (May peace be upon him) wearing thin clothes. The Apostle of Allah (peace be upon him) turned his attention from her. He said: 'O Asma', when a woman reaches the age of menstruation, it does not suit her that she displays her parts of body except this and this, and he pointed to his face and hands.'" (3523 Sahi Muslim & Bukhari)

In other words, her younger sister came before the Prophet in a semi-sheer gown through which the shape of her body was visible. The Prophet turned his head aside and said, "Only this and this should be visible," while pointing to his face and hands. Scholars have taken this story to mean that all Muslim women should cover themselves, leaving only their face and hands visible, even though most scholars also agree that this is a weak hadith, meaning its transmission cannot definitively be accounted for.

Whether you wear a head-scarf and fully cover yourself, or whether you just dress modestly, or even whether you wear shorts and a tank-top, no one has the prerogative to judge whether you are a 'good' Muslim or not. God is interested in the sincerity of your intentions and actions. While the Quran and life and sayings of the Prophet Muhammad are there to guide you - only you can choose the manner in which you live your life as a Muslim. If you are more concerned about what is in your head rather than what is covering your head, you won't go too far wrong. Islam stresses the inherent equality of the sexes, thereby encouraging you to view your peers as individual people based upon their characters and minds, not just as physical objects of sexual attraction.

Why Do YOU Wear Hijab?

The most common answers to this question were:

- My parents make me.

- I think it looks cool.

- My religion tells me to – I have to wear one if I'm a Muslim.

- It's easier to be a Muslim when I wear one.

- To be modest.

Farha (15), Illinois: "I wear hijab because not only does it cover your body, but it also shows how much you respect yourself."

97

Anonymous (14), Illinois: "It was rather a peer pressure thing. Everyone around me was wearing a hijab, so I wanted to also. But now I know the full importance of it. It's to cover your beauty."

Fathim (15), Illinois: "I like people to talk to me for my mind, not my body."

Why Don't YOU Wear Hijab?

The most common answers to this question were:

- I don't believe that God wants us to cover our hair.
- My mother doesn't.
- It's hot and uncomfortable.
- People will stare at me.
- I don't feel that my religion requires it.

Anonymous (15), Illinois: "At some point I was going to start, but then I said to myself, 'Some people who wear scarves aren't always the greatest Muslims.' People who don't wear scarves can also be good Muslims."

Mannan (12), Texas: "Because I'm a boy, not a girl!"

Rabia (14), Illinois: "I believe that a person should pray, fast, and work on the inside before the outside. So until I lose my bad habits, wearing a hijab doesn't seem right to me. I would feel hypocritical. Hopefully, I plan on wearing one."

Mehenaz (14), Ohio: "I don't think I'm ready for it. However, I respect girls who wear it."

Anonymous (13), Arizona: "Because God gave us hair – why should we hide it?"

ℬe honest...

- Do you judge people by what they wear?
- Do you assume someone who wears a hijab is more religious than you?
- Do you sometimes pretend you're not a Muslim?
- Do you choose your clothing in order to gain acceptance?
- Do you disagree with your parents on issues of clothing?
- Do you worry more about what you're wearing or what you're thinking?

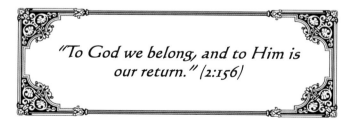

"To God we belong, and to Him is our return." [2:156]

NOTES

CHAPTER 13

Cultural Confusion
Examples of 'Muslim' Culture

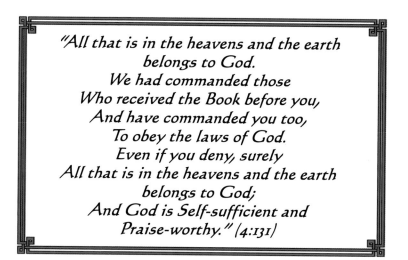

*"All that is in the heavens and the earth
belongs to God.
We had commanded those
Who received the Book before you,
And have commanded you too,
To obey the laws of God.
Even if you deny, surely
All that is in the heavens and the earth
belongs to God;
And God is Self-sufficient and
Praise-worthy." (4:131)*

What is culture? (No, it's not opera or fancy French restaurants.) Culture is a reflection of the traditions passed down within a family, community, or country. It may differ from place to place, and there is rarely a 'right' or 'wrong' culture (except for certain reprehensible acts like murder, rape, theft, etc., which are condemned in any culture.) Culture can be as simple as the language you speak, the food you eat, and the clothes you wear, or as complex as the way you celebrate your birthday or the way you handle a death in the family. Confusion arises when your culture (traditions) differs from your neighbor's, and you can't decide who's right and who's wrong. Does Muslim culture clash with American culture? Is there such a thing as a Muslim culture?

As a teenager, you probably feel an overpowering urge to fit in among your peers. Safety lies in numbers, so you try to keep a low profile by dressing like everyone around you (alright, you avoid the goth look and ignore the unwashed slob look too), sounding like everyone around you (it becomes second nature to change your accent/vocabulary between home and school), and acting like everyone around you. There's nothing wrong with melting into the crowd, but what do you do when you feel that everyone around you is doing the wrong thing? There are definitely times in your life when you have to assert your independence, especially when your conscience is beating you over the head and warning bells are ringing in your ears! Be mature for your age and avoid the following actions if you can: cheating, picking on unpopular kids, stealing, gossiping unnecessarily, shoplifting, bullying, cursing to sound cool, sleeping around to seem

cool, going into debt to look cool. Stop worrying about trying to be so cool!

Behavior that is perfectly acceptable at home may be out of place at school, and vice versa. Maybe your family likes to enjoy their evening meal seated on a clean sheet on the floor – don't try this in the school cafeteria unless you want footprints on your food. Do you normally dispense with cutlery and just dig right into your food using your fingers? Again, unless it's fried chicken, pizza, or hamburgers on the menu, you probably want to pick up that fork instead of limbering up your fingers.

Confusion sometimes arises when you're not sure what to do. If you find yourself in a situation where you're honestly clueless, just look around you and imitate your neighbor. Stand up and cheer when your team scores a touchdown, even if you have no idea what a touchdown is. Sit down and keep quiet when your class is watching an educational movie (heckling the actors may be the norm in your house, but don't forget that you're in school now.) You'll feel more accepted by your peers if you accommodate and adjust to your surroundings. That doesn't mean you become a clone of your best friend, but that you imitate just enough to fit in, without compromising your values or your identity.

> *"Among other signs of His is the creation of the heavens and the earth, and the variety of your tongues and complexions." [30:22]*

Examples of Muslim food...

- Pizza and hamburgers
- Shwarmas/gyros (roast lamb/chicken in pita bread)
- Rice and curry
- Chinese food
- Italian food
- Fruit and vegetables

Examples of Muslim clothes...

- T-shirt and jeans
- Skirts, dresses, long gowns
- Shalwar Kameez
- Suit/Jacket and tie
- Shorts, capris, etc.

Examples of Muslim languages...

- English
- Arabic
- French
- Urdu
- Malay
- Spanish
- Russian
- Chinese
- Esperanto

See the pattern?? There's no such thing as 'Muslim' food or 'Muslim' clothing per se. Sure, Indonesian Muslims prefer noodles while Pakistani Muslims enjoy rice, but as long as the food is halal, anything goes. Enjoy whatever cuisine takes your fancy. Don't label anyone by the food they eat, the language they speak, or the clothing they wear.

Books For the Culturally Confused

Born Confused by Tanuja Desai Hidier
- A hilarious account of a Hindu-Indian teenage girl's journey to acceptance of her own ethnicity in America.

Funny in Farsi by Firoozeh Dumas
- Funny in English, too! Read about Firoozeh's adventures in America.

West of Jordan by Laila Halaby
- Looks at the lives of four Arab-American cousins torn between Jordan, Arizona, and California.

Spiritualized by Mark Healy
- A beautifully put together account of fifteen teens' spiritual journeys.

Dahling, If You Luv Me, Would You Please, Please Smile by Rukhsana Khan
- Zainab craves a pair of Lucky jeans in order to be accepted by her school, but then realizes that she wants to be accepted for herself.

American Muslims by Asma Gull Hasan
- A non-fiction account of the challenges facing Muslims in America—issues include dating, marriage, and assimilation.

White Teeth by Zadie Smith

- Culture clash in London is depicted through two generations of Bengali/British families.

House of Sand and Fog by Andre Dubus III

- A poignant memoir of an Iranian family's struggle to adjust to life in San Francisco.

Interpreter of Maladies by Jhumpa Lahiri

- A collection of short stories chronicling love and loss between India and America.

The Hero's Walk by Anita Rau Badami

- A mesmerizing story of an Indian family with branches in Vancouver and India.

Sister of My Heart by Chitra Banerjee Divakaruni

- Traditional Indian values are juxtaposed against the American quest for self-fulfillment. A story of two women who take different paths in life.

An American Brat by Bapsi Sidhwa

- The adventures of a Pakistani teenager on a three-month holiday in America.

My Sister's Voices – Teenage Girls of Color Speak Out by Iris Jacob

- An amazing collection of writings that sums up the issues that we all face in today's multicultural world.

Are You Culturally Confident?

1. When your mom shows up in a traditional Indonesian outfit at Back-to-School night, you
   a) Run away when she calls you to sit next to her.
   b) Proudly explain what the outfit is called to everyone within a 10-mile radius
   c) Do what you always do: chat with your friends until it's time to go.

2. Your Iranian cousin has just moved here, and he's attending your schol. When he runs up to you speaking Farsi, you
   a) Shut him in the nearest broom closet.
   b) Start up a long conversation with him in Farsi, too.
   c) Reply in English, and show him where the bathrooms are.
   d) You don't have a clue what he's saying because you don't speak Farsi — your parents never taught you.

107

3. A television repairman has just come to your house while your mom is in the middle of cooking up a strong-smelling curry. As he sniffs the air curiously, you:
   a) Frantically spray air freshener everywhere – including on the curry.
   b) Offer to prepare a plate of it for him.
   c) Decide now would be a good time to slink off to your room.
   d) Loudly ask whether your science project concoction simmering on the stove is ready yet.

4. You're taking your relatives (who are visiting from a little village in India) to the mall. When you see some people from school approaching you, you
   a) Dash into the nearest store – never mind that it's the store that only sells Star Trek stuff.
   b) Hold Aunty's hand while she 'oohs' and 'ahhs' over the neon lights, ignoring the curious stares she's attracting from your school friends.
   c) Nonchalantly stroll away from your relatives and pretend to be engrossed in the latest display of baby clothes.
   d) Introduce them to your friends – you're proud that you are able to switch effortlessly between two different cultures.

Interpret Your Answers...
(Ethnic expert or culturally clueless?)

There are no right or wrong answers (well, ok, you shouldn't really lock your cousin into the broom closet at school!), but in general, your answers probably reflect the level of cultural confidence you feel. Whether you're Jewish, Christian, Muslim, or an atheist, sometimes your religious beliefs will lead you down a different path from the majority of your peers. When you add the spice of a different ethnic or racial background into the recipe, the end result may be deliciously different.

Embrace your individual identity while acknowledging the validity that each of us has to think our own thoughts, follow our own paths, and pursue our own goals. Most teens aspire to achieve success in their life – whether it is defined by money, power, fame, or peace is entirely a personal choice. Don't allow society to label you unless you truly feel that the label fits. (Do you even need a label?) You're a person, not a can of soup on a shelf in the grocery store of life.

NOTES

CHAPTER 14

Inventions from the Muslim World

Where Did Algebra Come From, Anyway?

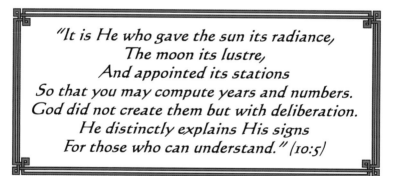

"It is He who gave the sun its radiance,
The moon its lustre,
And appointed its stations
So that you may compute years and numbers.
God did not create them but with deliberation.
He distinctly explains His signs
For those who can understand." (10:5)

Did you ever wonder who invented algebra? Or how ships navigate? Or even how that watch on your wrist operates? Well, these are all inventions that arose from the Muslim world. Between the 8th and 10th centuries, classical Islamic civilization spread throughout the Middle East, Asia, and Europe. While Europe and much of the Western World was passing through what is known as the 'Dark Ages,' scholars universally recognize that the Islamic civilization kept the torch of learning alight. By translating, preserving, and elucidating upon research in countless fields, Islamic scholars played a critical role in Europe's transition from the Dark Ages to the Renaissance. Muslim scholars adopted the experimental method of testing their hypotheses and observations rather than the Socratic method that was commonly used at the time. Their achievement of translating earlier scientific works by the Greeks, Chinese, and Indians into Arabic enabled them to pursue innovative avenues of thought and original research. This preservation through translation furthered many of the heretofore theoretical sciences of medicine, astronomy, and mathematics, to name a few. Western European civilization absorbed this body of Islamic thought, and through subsequent translation into Latin and English, laid the framework for much of modern Western science and philosophy. The principles of scientific investigation encouraged by Muslim thinkers extended across many disciplines, from art, architecture, and astronomy, continuing through the alphabet to end with zoology!

In 763 AD, Baghdad became the capital of the Muslim world. It was a bustling city at the crossroads of the major trade routes between Asia and Europe. Scholars flocked to this city to offer their services to the rulers and to further their knowledge through exchanges with learned travelers, and eventually established a 'House of Wisdom'. This institute served a two-fold purpose. One was the systematic translation of Greek scientific and philosophical works into Arabic. The other was primarily as a research institution

undertaking ground-breaking work in various fields. From Baghdad, knowledge spread outward into the rest of the Muslim empire, encouraging original thinking through investigative techniques in cities as far away as Cordoba, Seville, Cairo, and New Delhi.

Al-Azhar University, founded in 972 AD in Cairo, Egypt, is the world's oldest university and remains one of the most famous sites for original research into the field of Islam. It concentrates on both the study of the Quran as well as the study of modern science. Countless other seats of learning sprang up in Syria, Spain, India, Turkey, and throughout the Muslim world. In addition to their many contributions in the sciences, Muslims also left a legacy of art and architecture still visible to this day.

As Islam spread, it absorbed the myriad cultural influences it encountered. For example, mosques retained their overall simplicity of purpose, but the addition of a dome came about through integrating Byzantine architectural traditions. Similarly, mosques in Iran soon included intricate tile-work common to the region. The Taj Mahal is perhaps the most famous example of Islamic architecture in Asia, while the Dome of the Rock in Jerusalem displays beautiful mosaics as a legacy from the earlier

Taj Mahal

The Dome of the Rock

Greeks and Romans in the region. Islamic art ranges from calligraphy to textiles to miniature paintings and can be seen in museums throughout the world.

Inventors and Their Inventions/ Innovations

- **Kutbi** – watch
- **Abdul Hasan** – telescope
- **Ibn Yunus** – pendulum
- **Unknown Muslims** – mariner's compass
- **Al-Khawarizmi** – advances in algebra
- **Ibn al-Haitham** – the "Father of Optics"
- **Ibn Sina (Avicenna)** – Philosopher/Physician, wrote *Canon of Medicine,* the standard medical text used in Europe for 7 centuries.
- **Jabbir bin-Hayyan** – advances in chemistry
- **Omar Khayyam** – author of the *Rubaiyat,* a work of poetry
- **Muslim mathematicians** – 'Arabic' numerals, which replaced Roman numerals (1,2,3 instead of I, II, III).
- **Ibn Rushd (Averroes)** – philosopher who reconciled Aristotle with Islam.

The list goes on and on. These are just a few examples of Muslim contributions to our modern world.

CHAPTER 15

Peer Pressure
Don't Worry, I Feel It, Too

> *"O men, We created you from a male and female,*
> *And formed you into nations and tribes*
> *That you may recognise each other.*
> *He who has more integrity*
> *Has indeed greater honor with God.*
> *Surely God is All-knowing and*
> *Well-informed."* (49:13)

The community of Muslims all over the world is referred to as an 'ummah,' a community. While the Quran specifically refers to the diversity among man as a strength, individual citizens sometimes choose to emphasize their superiority over one another based upon the color of their skin, their education, or their wealth. These arbitrary prejudices have no place in Islam, which stresses the inherent equality of all people. Muslims are taught not to pass judgment on each other as God is the ultimate judge of us all.

Teenagers face unique challenges and opportunities, especially in high schools. The innocence of childhood where friendships are based upon such simple factors as liking your neighbor's lunchbox, for instance, or automatically assuming that the person sitting next to you will be your best friend (remember when you considered the person who ate lunch with you the most important person in the whole school?!), is replaced with more complicated decisions based upon appearance, wardrobe, and 'coolness.' Fitting in with the crowd becomes increasingly important as teens struggle to define themselves within their school community, their new 'ummah.'

What happens when you feel like an outsider? Your religion may set you apart at times, but it can also provide you with the confidence to stand apart from the crowd and distinguish yourself in other ways. Rather than worrying so much about finding acceptance in a group with questionable values, surround yourself with people who share your morals. Join a sports team or a club that interests you. Above all, keep busy and motivated, and you'll find that the differences you worried about may disappear as your peers get to know you better. By standing firm on issues that matter to you, you'll gain the respect of many people who secretly feel the same way you do, but don't have the confidence to declare their convictions.

Teen Solutions to Negative Peer Pressure

- **Mentors** – college students or adults in fields that interest you.

- **Internships** – a great way to investigate future careers.

- **Part-time jobs** – earn $$$!

- **Travel** – meet new people, see new places, experience new lifestyles.

- **Volunteer** – feel good about working while being unpaid and unselfish.

- **Study abroad** – immerse yourself in a different culture.

- **Sports** – build athleticism, ability, and team spirit.

- **Youth groups** – informal and non-judgmental groups offering peer support and discussion.

- **Community service** – give back to your community.

- **Behavioral contract** – outline permitted activities with your parents.

How Do YOU Handle Peer Pressure?

Muslim Teens Speak Out...

Fariha (15), Illinois: "Pretty well. I believe whatever is best for me, I will do. I could care less about whether people like it or not."

Arooj (14), Ohio: "I don't believe there is such a thing. As long as a person has strength and good intentions, then inshallah, they will be able to handle any situation."

Anonymous (17), Illinois: "Staying away from people who might pressure me."

Asif (15), Texas: "Walk away."

Maya (11), Arizona: "I handle it well because it doesn't pressure me."

118

Muslim Teens' Role Models

- Prophet Muhammad, because he wanted to please God.

- My mother, because she struggles to be the best Muslim.

- Aisha bint Abu Bakr, because she was very clever.

- My cousin Nazeef, because he is a very sincere Muslim.

- Khadija, because she supported her husband.

- Anyone who is better than me spiritually

- My parents and grandparents, because they taught me many things.

- No one.

- My grandmother, because she's very old and has a hard time moving around, but she never misses a salat (complete with wudu).

- Mr. Meyers, my English teacher, because he's a convert and has a totally strong faith, yet he is normal and not all fanatical right-wing/Taliban.

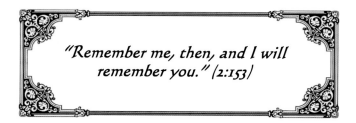

"Remember me, then, and I will remember you." (2:153)

Problems and Solutions

Stereotypes	*or*	The 'Real' You
Trends	*or*	Being Yourself
Cliques	*or*	Finding True Friends
Acceptance	*or*	Confidence
Identity Crisis	*or*	Spiritual Strength
Rebellion	*or*	Communication
Conflict	*or*	Consensus
Doubt	*or*	Trust
Ignorance	*or*	Knowledge
Ostracism	*or*	Assimilation
Antagonism	*or*	Understanding
Boredom	*or*	Positive Attitudes
Racism	*or*	Empowerment
Argument	*or*	Resolution
Question of Trust	*or*	Responsibility

Do You Think It's Easy Being A Muslim in America?

No, because...

- There are too many temptations.
- After 9/11 everyone thinks Muslims are terrorists.
- People stare at Muslims in headscarves.
- I'm not allowed to do the same things my friends do.
- The American culture is too different.
- There are many racist people.
- Too much peer pressure.
- Too many distractions like TV, music, movies etc.
- Too much discrimination.
- It's very, very difficult!

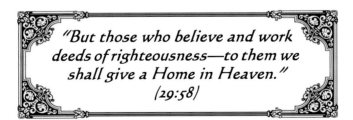

"But those who believe and work deeds of righteousness—to them we shall give a Home in Heaven."
(29:58)

Do You Think It's Easy Being A Muslim in America?

Yes, because...

- There's freedom of religion.

- If you fear God, you can live anywhere you want.

- We have freedom of speech while some Muslim countries don't.

- I have strong faith and lots of Muslim friends.

- I realize the differences between Muslims and non-Muslims.

- God will always help us.

- After 9/11 some non-Muslim Americans sympathize with us, too.

- A lot of people in America are becoming Muslims.

- In America, nobody really cares who you are.

- You can do whatever you put your mind to – no one ever got into Heaven without struggling!

- It depends on you, not your surroundings.

CONCLUSION

Religion is a complex topic. Whether you choose to ignore it entirely, complaisantly accept your parents' version, or explore it for yourself – the choice is yours. The big questions of 'Who am I?' or 'What's my purpose in life?' or even 'Is there a Heaven or Hell?' are rarely answered to anyone's complete satisfaction. However, delving into the study of religion can point you in the direction of finding some answers. Whichever path you choose, remember that you're not alone – millions of people continue to search for guides to help them live lives of happiness, fulfillment, and inner peace. Islam can truly be a way to find peace through submission to God, just as Judaism, Christianity, and numerous other faiths continue to educate and enlighten their followers. If you follow a straight path of obedience to God and live your life in the knowledge that God is always aware of your thoughts and actions, you will find happiness and a sense of peace wherever you go.

APPENDIX

The Questionnaire

First Name:_____ Age:_____ Male/Female:_____

Status (circle one):
Full-time Islamic School   Weekend Only   None

Please be as honest as possible in answering the following questions. Feel free to expand on any of your answers on the back page. Thank you for your assistance in compiling this handbook for Muslim Teens!

FAITH

1. What does being a Muslim mean to you?

2. Do you think that the 5 Pillars of Islam summarize the faith?

3. Do you pray? If so, how often? If not regularly, why not?

4. Do you fast during Ramadan? If so, how often, and when did you begin?

5. How do you celebrate Eid?

6. Do you give Zakat?

7. Do you anticipate doing Hajj?

8. Why are you a Muslim?

TEEN ISSUES

1. What are your thoughts on the 4 'D's (dating, dancing, drinking, and drugs)?

2. Who is your Muslim role model? Why?

3. What is your biggest issue/concern?

4. What is your parents' biggest issue/concern?

5. Do you think that it is easy being a Muslim in America?

6. How do you handle peer pressure?

7. Are most of your friends Muslims or non-Muslims?

8. Do you wear hijab? What are your reasons for or against it?

9. What is your idea of modesty?

10. Do your parents 'censor' your friends, TV-watching, music etc?

11. Have you ever felt discriminated against due to your religion?

12. What are your goals (academic, religious, personal)?

BIBLIOGRAPHY

Azim, Syed Aftab. *The Pilgrimage.* Karachi: Pakistan International Airlines, 1985.

Cook, Michael. *The Koran.* Oxford: Oxford University Press, 2000.

Haddad, Yvonne Yazbeck & Adair T. Lummis. *Islamic Values In The United States.* New York: Oxford University Press, Inc. 1987.

Hasan, Asma Gull. *American Muslims.* New York: Continuum International Publishing Group, 2000.

Lang, Jeffrey. *Even Angels Ask.* Beltsville: Amana Publications, 1997.

Lunde, Paul. *Islam.* New York: Dorling Kindersly Publishing, Inc. 2002.

Wolfe, Michael. *the Hadj.* New York: Grove Press, 1993.

Wolfe, Michael ed. *Taking Back Islam.* Rodale Inc. and Beliefnet, Inc. 2002.

Yasmine   Dilara   Imran

MEET THE AUTHORS

Dilara Hafiz was born in Karachi, Pakistan. She holds degrees from Johns Hopkins University and the London School of Economics. She has drawn upon her years of teaching weekend Islamic school, lecturing about Islam, and the experience of raising Muslim teenagers to contribute to *The American Muslim Teenager's Handbook*.

Imran Hafiz is a freshman at Brophy College Preparatory in Phoenix, Arizona. He's involved in Speech & Debate and Weapons of Mass Percussion (a djembe drum club). He enjoys reading, playing video games, and arguing over politics. He plays the guitar, piano, and drums as well as various tribal instruments.

Yasmine Hafiz is a junior at Xavier College Preparatory in Phoenix, Arizona. She loves reading, listening to music, sewing, and traveling. She also enjoys going to the library and would like to learn more about philosophy and art history.

Hamid, Dilara, Yasmine, and Imran live in Paradise Valley, Arizona.

NOTES

NOTES

NOTES